John Lathern

The Macedonian Cry

a voice from the lands of Brahma and Buddha, Africa and isles of the sea and a plea

for missions

John Lathern

The Macedonian Cry
a voice from the lands of Brahma and Buddha, Africa and isles of the sea and a plea for missions

ISBN/EAN: 9783337246716

Printed in Europe, USA, Canada, Australia, Japan

Cover: Foto ©Lupo / pixelio.de

More available books at **www.hansebooks.com**

THE MACEDONIAN CRY;

A VOICE FROM

THE LANDS OF BRAHMA AND BUDDHA,

AFRICA AND ISLES OF THE SEA,

AND

A PLEA FOR MISSIONS.

By REV. JOHN LATHERN.

"There stood a man of Macedonia, and prayed him, saying, Come over into Macedonia and help us."

TORONTO:
WILLIAM BRIGGS, 78 & 80 KING ST., EAST.
MONTREAL: C. W. COATES.   HALIFAX: S. F. HUESTIS

ENTERED, according to the Act of the Parliament of Canada, in the year one thousand eight hundred and eighty-four, by WM. BRIGGS, in the Office of the Minister of Agriculture.

TO HONORED

BRETHREN OF MISSIONARY DEPUTATIONS,

AS INTERPRETERS OF

THE MACEDONIAN CRY,

THIS

PLEA FOR MISSIONS

IS RESPECTFULLY INSCRIBED

BY THE

AUTHOR.

PREFACE.

THE duty, privilege, and encouragement of Christians to send the Gospel to the unenlightened nations of the earth, was the subject of Dr. John Harris' "Great Commission," and of Dr. Richard Winter Hamilton's "Christian Missions." It is not proposed in the following pages, and indeed the attempt were superfluous, to traverse the ground taken by those gifted essayists.

An effort has been made to write rather from the standpoint of 1883, to exhibit the character of Oriental religious systems, to delineate some features of an uncivilized heathenism, to summarize missionary facts and results, and to urge an earnest plea for Protestant missions—the glory of this nineteenth century.

An experience of anniversaries has shewn the advantage of definite views in regard to the authority, demands, and possibilities of missions; central ideas, around which new facts and illustrative incidents may be readily grouped; and should this essay be found at all helpful in the direction indicated, a main purpose of its publication will have been gained.

J. L.

CONTENTS.

I.
A Man of Macedonia: Help for Heathendom 9

II.
Civilized Heathenism: Hinduism and the Hindus 31

III.
Civilized Heathenism: Buddhism and the Buddhists 59

IV.
Uncivilized Heathenism: Africa and Isles of the Sea ... 85

V.
Modern Missions and Mission Stations 119

VI.
Progress and Results of Missions 159

VII.
Missionary Methods and Agencies 185

VIII.
Go, or Send: the Commission 211

IX.
Missions and Money 233

X.
The World for Christ 253

Appendix 277

"Souls in heathen darkness lying,
   Where no light has broken through,
Souls that Jesus bought by dying,
   Whom his soul in travail knew—
      Thousand voices
   Call us o'er the waters blue.

"Haste, O haste, and spread the tidings
   Wide to earth's remotest strand;
Let no brother's bitter chidings
   Rise against us when we stand
      In the judgment,
   From some far, forgotten land."

             —*Mrs. C. F. Alexander.*

THE MACEDONIAN CRY.

I.

A MAN OF MACEDONIA: HELP FOR HEATHENDOM.

THE call from Macedonia was an important incident of St. Paul's second missionary tour. Through the gates of Syria and Cilicia, he and Silvanus passed up into a rough region formed by the central table-land of Asia Minor. For a time, they travelled by the signal posts of recently-formed missions. Timotheus joined them at Derbe. Churches were founded in Phrygia and Galatia. They passed into Mysia, and essayed to go into Bithynia, but the Spirit of Jesus suffered them not. Uncertain in regard to the immediate future, these heaven-guided messengers of the cross then turned aside to Troas. Here they trod on more than historic ground. Each legendary spot had been immortalized in the best strains of Greece. It was almost impossible for any one of the intellectual caste and culture of St. Paul to be insensible to the romantic associations that clustered so richly around that classic coast. But, in the inspired narrative, there is no allusion to Homer's heroes, or to Ilion's towers. The mission of the cross had become an absorbing and consuming passion. He was determined to know nothing among men "save Jesus Christ and him crucified." Across the straits to the north-west the eye would rest on an outline of distant Macedonian hills. There is the landmark of an unvisited Europe. That western continent is the home of the polished Greeks and powerful Romans. Deeper in the heart of its mighty forests are noble but still uncivilized races, destined to future greatness, and to grand and stirring action on the theatre of human history. Was not that unknown territory comprised in the commission? Could the mystery and misery of Occidental heathenism be pierced and dispelled? Ought not an attempt at once to be made to break ground on a new soil? Such, as, from the harbor of Troas or musing along the shore, he glanced to distant and lofty isle and peak, must have been the direction of the Apostle's thought. It may have been one of those magnificent sunsets, such as modern travellers have described. In the far distance, reflecting the radiance of evening splendor, Mount Athos would be visible from the Asiatic shore. Its colossal peak, seen as "a mass of burnished gold," might well look like "some vast angel" beckoning him "to carry the good tidings to the west." Thus probably the great missionary lingered by those Ægean waters until the shadows of night deepened over land and sea. There would, therefore, be a kind of mental preparation for supernatural intimation. "And a vision appeared to Paul in the night; there stood a man of Macedonia and prayed him, saying, Come over into Macedonia and help us." The voice that spake in that dream, mental impression, or visible manifestation, could scarcely be any occasion of surprise. The man of the night vision was the representative of a European population, and of all western heathendom. A Divine call took the form of one of the people providentially prepared to receive the message of salvation. An appeal was made for help. It was the utterance of a deep-felt sense of need, and of an unconscious preparation for the reception of a gospel message. There could be no doubt as to the kind of help that was needed. Response was immediate. There was no demur or delay on the ground of heathen at home, or of the yet unconverted thousands in Syria and Asia Minor. The Apostles of Jesus Christ understood their commission to mean that the glad tidings of salvation should be made known at the earliest possible time to all lands and peoples of the earth. What, if St. Paul had refused to be guided by the Spirit of Jesus, and had selected a Bithynian field of labor? Had he, when summoned to Europe, refused a reponse to the Macedonian cry, how different would have been the early history of the Church! But is there not still an imperative call to special work? Ought not ministers of the gospel, as did the first great missionaries, without regard to personal preferences, freely and promptly to accept a home or foreign field of effort? Not a moment was lost at Troy. Memories of "human gods and godlike men" had no potent spell to bind them to that starry shore. A Macedonian passage was at once secured, and soon they were bounding past the "sprinkled isles" and across the blue waves of the narrow sea. A beloved physician, St. Luke, the representative of medical missions, seems to have embarked with them, and hence the change of *person* from the third to the first: "And after he had seen the vision, immediately we endeavored to go into Macedonia, assuredly gathering that the Lord had called us for to preach the gospel unto them. Therefore, loosing from Troas, we came with a straight course to Samothracia, and the next day to Neapolis; and from thence to Philippi, which is the chief city of that part of Macedonia, and a colony."

The Apostle Paul had a knowledge of the heathenism of Europe, that enabled him rightly to interpret the Macedonian cry.

The Ægean sea was almost the sanctuary of ancient superstition. Ida's wooded heights were peopled with divinities. Fountain and stream, pine-clad gorge and rocky promontory, were haunted by shadowy legend, or associated with stirring and storied deeds. Surrounded by such symbols and memorials, about to enter proud and magnificent cities where heathenism sat enthroned, the mind of the Apostle must have been directed to the darker aspects of this subject. No one ever more acutely studied or stated the evils of a prevalent idolatrous system. He came to comprehend its most characteristic developments. Something of classic civilization we know from other sources. The researches of Leake and Wood and Schliemann in Asia Minor, Ephesus, the Troad and Greek peninsula, and the extended excavations in Pompeii, indicate the resolve of modern explorers; determined, from its own records and remains, to trace out the facts and features of paganism. But "he who would see but for a moment and afar off to what the Gentile world had sunk, at the very period when Christianity began to spread, may form some faint and shuddering conception from the picture drawn of it in the Epistle to the Romans."* It is from the pen of St. Paul that we can learn the whole dark story:

" Because that, when they knew God, they glorified him not as God, neither were thankful; but became vain in their imaginations and their foolish heart was darkened. Professing themselves to be wise, they became fools, and changed the glory of the incorruptible God into an image made like to corruptible man, and to birds, and four-footed beasts, and creeping things. Wherefore God also gave them up to uncleanness through the lusts of their own hearts, to dishonor their own bodies between themselves: who changed the truth of God into a lie, and worshipped and served the creature more than the creator, who is blessed forever. Amen. For this cause God gave

---

* Farrar's *Seekers after God*, p. 36.

them up to vile affections; for even their women did change the natural use into that which is against nature: and likewise also the men, leaving the natural use of the women, burned in lust one toward another; men with men working that which is unseemly, and receiving in themselves that recompense of their error which was meet. And even as they did not like to retain God in their knowledge, God gave them over to a reprobate mind, to do those things which are not convenient; being filled with all unrighteousness, fornication, wickedness, covetousness, maliciousness; full of envy, murder, debate, deceit, malignity; whisperers, backbiters, haters of God, despiteful, proud, boasters, inventors of evil things, disobedient to parents, without natural affection, implacable, unmerciful; who knowing the judgment of God, that they which commit such things are worthy of death, not only do the same, but have pleasure in them that do them."

Such, according to inspired delineation, was the paganism of Europe and the East; its atheism, licentiousness, cruelties, and nameless corruptions. The indictment is tremendous, and allegation is black and burning. Corruption is laid bare to its very heart. Not a gleam of fancy, or of poetic imaginativeness, relieves the relentless process. In the severe and searching light of God's infinite purity, unrighteousness reveals its most repulsive aspects. Is it any wonder, impelled by a feeling of holy indignation, that the Apostle put upon that foul system the stamp and stigma of loathing and of utter abhorrence?

The period of Roman life and civilization, to which this awful passage has specific reference, has been frequently and glowingly panegyrized. It was the superb Augustan age. The eloquence and victories of Cicero and Cæsar were yet a proud remembrance. Mantuan melodies still lingered in the air. It was in many respects a wonderful time. A complex civilization had brought its forces and appliances to bear upon some of the finest material the world has ever seen. Genius had scarcely more than passed the zenith of its splendor. Intellect was still proud and brilliant. Life was voluptuous. There was opulence to repletion, and everything to minister to the sensual nature. Beauty was deified. Even around the altars and idolatries of that time there was a marvellous and fascinating combination of majesty and grace, of science and taste. Whatever man could do without the living God was carried up to the point of perfection. But that structure of polished paganism had darker and more repelling aspects. It was unspiritual and immoral. Faith that saves, like the luminous flame, diffuses splendor; but, like mist and murk, superstition deepens the shadows of the night. Established religion had exhibited a constantly deteriorating and downward process. The Pantheon in Rome was worse even than the Parthenon of Greece. Pagan gods were the patrons and prompters of crime and pollution. Deities were such as lust demanded. Faith was lost, and purity and patriotism were gone. Oriental superstitions and pollutions steeped and saturated the Occident. "Orontes overflowed the Tiber."

In regard to the character of that century, we have contemporary and competent witness. Seneca sorrowed for the degeneracy of the times. Innocence, according to the testimony of this accomplished philosopher, had ceased to exist. "Discarding respect for all that is good and sacred, lust rushes on wherever it will."* From the capital a stream of pollution flowed out into provincial cities; but with fresh and fouler accumulation it was rapidly poured back into the main reservoir. Humanity, morally and spiritually, was at its worst and sorest need. The world by wisdom knew not God.

In mediæval exploration, amongst the ruins of Pompeii, Lorenzo and Leo are said to have discovered altar lamps. Once these had contained sacred fire, but the oil was gone, and they could not now be relighted. Such was the condition of classic science and philosophy, when Christianity first flashed its radiance across the dark expanse. Flame was extinct. Hope was dead. There was scarcely a solitary ray of

---

* "Modern unbelief complains that St. Paul has characterized the social morality of the pagan world in terms of undue severity. Yet St. Paul does not exceed the specific charges of Tacitus, of Suetonius, of Juvenal, of Seneca, that is to say of writers that had no theological interest in misrepresenting or exaggerating the facts which they deplore. When Tacitus summarizes the moral condition of paganism by his exhaustive phrase, *corrumpere et corrumpi*, he more than covers the sorrowing invective of the Apostle."—CANON LIDDON, *Bampton Lectures*, 1866, p. 139.

even a heathen faith to relieve the dreariness and monotony of prevalent materialism. Moral miasma brooded over the scene. Every spiritual aspiration was chilled and checked.

> "On that hard pagan world, disgust
> And secret loathing fell;
> Deep weariness and sated lust
> Made human life a hell."

"No wonder," says Dr. Brown, in his exposition of Romans, "that, thus sick and dying as was this poor humanity of ours under the highest earthly culture, its many-voiced cry for the balm in Gilead and the Physician there—*Come over and help us*—pierced the hearts of the missionaries of the cross, and made them not ashamed of the gospel of Christ."

The question of heathen *accountability* comes to the front in this connection. The biblical truth that all men must be judged by the deeds done in the body has been luminously represented as "the pillar of fire" which constitutes "the supernatural vanguard of Christian missions." Inspiration is clear and cleaving in its enunciation and enforcement of this solemn and profoundly awful subject. Hence the appalling passage in which St. Paul depicts heathenism. Strong relief is sought. The main argument is designed to shut up a sinful and guilty world to the mercy of God, to demonstrate the necessity of a Divine and remedial scheme, and to enforce the sublime doctrine of salvation through grace. They who have not received a written law, the revelation of truth, are under another and clearly-defined dispensation. "For as many as have sinned without law, shall also perish without law: and as many as have sinned in the law, shall be judged by the law (for when the Gentiles, which have not the law, do by nature the things contained in the law, these having not the law are a law unto themselves: which shew the work of the law written in their hearts, their consciences also bearing witness, and their thoughts in the meanwhile accusing, or else excusing, one another); in the day when God shall judge the secrets of men, by Jesus Christ according to my gospel."

A supreme faculty of conscience has been implanted in the human soul. There is also a "true Light that lighteneth every man that cometh into the world." An inward law commends or condemns. Gracious illumination constitutes the measure of human responsibility; and, at the future and final tribunal, when the judgment shall be set, and the books opened, it must determine acceptance or rejection, salvation or exclusion. "But we are sure," affirms the Apostle, „that the judgment of God is according to truth, ag inst them that do such things."

Inspired reasoning lights up an abstruse and perplexing question, and reveals also an underlying and essential principle of missionary impulse and action. It enables us, when carried into the region of heathen life and experience, to grasp the significance of many a testimony. "When I remember," says the evangelist Sing, of the China inland mission, "how I sinned against the light which heaven gave to my nature, how I obeyed the selfish instincts of my soul, and was led astray by evil seductions, sinning against light, *I feel how guilty I was.*" The earlier part of the Epistle to the Romans was read by a Buddhist priest of Ceylon, in his own language. His main object at the outset was to obtain arguments for the refutation of Christianity. The first chapter astonished him beyond measure. Secret things from dark chambers of imagery, of which he had been cognizant, were brought to light. Sins that were sadly too common among his countrymen were comprised in the dark catalogue. There was a startling accuracy of delineation. Such is the unchanged character of heathenism, of its idolatries and consequent immoralities, that missionaries have been actually charged with the forgery of this terrible passage. Adherents of Oriental systems find it difficult to believe that so full and forcible a description could have been written at the commencement of the Christian era. The Singhalese student passed on to the second chapter, and there he encountered a new surprise. That account of the law written on the heart answered to actual and repeated experiences of life. Doing of wrong had often been a cause of remorseful feeling. Conscience must have been troubled. An unwelcome monitor had refused to be driven away, or silenced, at any moment. That witness of the heart could not be an evil thing; for it condemned the wrong, and approved the good. Against light and knowledge had sin been many times committed. There must be consequent guilt and liability to punishment. This universal law became the subject of repeated conversation with a missionary, whose acquaintance had been formed. The sequence of thought was in exact adaptation to the tastes and mental habits of the controversialist. His interest for a time centred in the close texture of the reasoning, and in the cogency and conclusiveness of the argument. But he began to find that a sharp arrow had pierced the joints of his tightened armour. Conviction of sin gradually deepened to genuine distress. "Is there any peace of conscience," he anxiously inquired, "any pardon of sin in the Christian religion?" It would be sufficient, in reply to that question of supreme interest and importance, to read passages from the same evangelical and glorious Epistle:

"I am not ashamed of the gospel of Christ: for it is the power of God unto salvation to every one that believeth." "Being justified freely by his grace, through the redemption that is in Christ Jesus: whom God hath set forth to be a propitiation through faith in his blood, to declare his righteousness for the remission of sins that are past." "Therefore being justified by faith, we have peace with God through our Lord Jesus Christ." "That as sin hath reigned unto death, even so might grace reign through righteousness, unto eternal life, by Jesus Christ our Lord."

The Macedonian cry has become the world's cry.

Modern heathenism is fully as dark and debasing, as polluted and miserable, as was that of Apostolic times. The man of Macedonia represents a perishing world. Night visions are renewed from age to age. Masses and millions of people are pleading for succour. In painful and piercing accents, they are ever saying, *Come over and help us.* The Rev. Wm. O. Simpson, during an evangelistic tour through Northern India, a few years ago, preached from the steps of an idol temple. The first proclamation of salvation through Jesus was thus made in a populous city. "Once," said a venerable-looking Brahman, putting his hand to his head, "this lock of hair was black as the raven's wing: now it is white as the snow on the summits of the Himalaya; and I have been waiting all these years to hear words like these."

> "Grown white with waiting! O brothers all!
> Is there for you in these words no call?
> Stirs there no pulse in your inmost soul,
> As by you these heart-waves of pleading roll?"

A thrilling appeal just now comes from the region of the Transvaal and the Molopo territory, in South Africa. In words of pathos and pain, an aged Baralong chief tells how he has looked and longed in vain, through many weary years, for the message and the ministry of the gospel of the Lord Jesus Christ. The Missionary Society, in which he trusted, had failed him. "Why," he asks, " have we been so long left? I have no hope now. When I am dead, and my nation is scattered, then, perhaps, when the opportunity is lost for ever, they will send a missionary."* Such a plaint is enough

---

* *Missionary Notices*, May, 1883.

to make the very stones cry out, in rebuke of the apathy of the Christian Church. Is not the heart-stricken Montsioa an unconscious representative of Africa's benighted millions of people?

But there is also the voice of this western continent, calling for help. A beam of light strikes the spiritual vision of a blind Indian in the wilds of Alaska. He has heard that Jesus Christ came into the world to save sinners; and the story of infinite love, imperfectly told by a wanderer of his own tribe, moves the heart as nothing else can do. Something more he must know of the wondrous fact of redeeming grace and mercy. Guided by another Indian, the eager inquirer starts out in search of light and help. Through mountain gorge and pathless forest, gliding along rivers unknown to song, as many suns rise and set, at a distance of *one thousand miles* the nearest mission station is reached, and the heart is made glad by tidings of great joy. Does not that Indian of the distant wilderness represent the dusky tribes of this continent, and other races of the unsaved pagan world, in the same sense that a man of Macedonia represented the idolatrous populations of Europe, and the heathendom of the time? From the ice-bound coast of Labrador to far-away and frozen Alaska, and from inland lake to polar sea, there comes a cry for help. Our country's voice is pleading. Home missionaries are needed. But the field is the world. The Macedonian appeal comes from every land. It crosses not only straits, but continents and oceans; wafted on the wings of every breeze, and borne on the bosom of every swelling billow. The idea finds expression in Heber's matchless missionary hymn:

> "From Greenland's icy mountains,
> From India's coral strand,
> Where Afric's sunny fountains
> Roll down their golden sand;
> From many an ancient river,
> From many a balmy plain,
> They call us to deliver
> Their land from error's chain."

Suppose for a moment that the Macedonian of St. Paul's vision, the Brahman of sultry India, or the African chief, Montsioa, was not the representative of a race or of the heathen world. Think of him as one man; an unsaved Cree or Kaffir, Hindu or Hottentot, Cossack or Tartar. Though rude in speech, and degraded to the dust, that man is redeemed by Christ, an heir of immortality. For him there must be a resurrection to eternal life, or to shame and everlasting contempt. At the bar of God destiny shall be determined according to the deeds done in the body. Is there not an imminent spiritual peril? Suppose, again, for the sake of illustration, that, with but a solitary exception, the whole heathen world had been converted to Christ, and that there was but one dark and unsaved idolater on the face of the earth. What shall be done to pluck that immortal soul as a brand from the burning, and to add one more gem to the Redeemer's radiant crowns? That soul in value outweighs the material magnificence of worlds on worlds. Would it be too much that an effort and expenditure equal to the aggregate of what is required for the work of the Church at home and of missions abroad, if nothing less would avail, should be employed for its salvation? Could it be any cause for surprise if there were silence and suspense in heaven itself, till the fate of that deathless soul were determined, or that ministering spirits should stand ready for any mission that might secure the last trophy of redeeming mercy? But the Macedonian is only a unit in the aggregate of the yet unsaved multitudes.

Think of the spiritual condition of the great mass of the world's teeming population, estimated at more than fourteen hundred million! A system of imposture, Mohammedanism, numbers over one hundred and seventy millions of adherents. Fully one-half of the people of the earth, including the Brahmans of India, the Buddhists of eastern and central Asia, and the dwellers of a few islands of the sea, are idolaters. They are doomed to darkness and the shadow of death, and in their blindness bow down to gods of wood and stone. The mass of these know nothing of God's reconciling mercy, or of the glad tidings of salvation. One can scarcely be surprised at the emotion which finds expression in the utterances of an earnest and eloquent advocate and exponent of missions and missionary policy: "As I coasted along Ceylon and the Malay peninsula and vast China day after day, I seemed to hear across the roar of the waves, the tur-

bulent sound of the billows of humanity, breaking
with a wail upon the stern coasts of our yet barbaric
days. Three hundred million billows in China, half
of them women, two hundred and fifty such billows
breaking on the shores of India, multitudes upon
multitudes coming out of the unseen and storming
across the ocean of time to break on the shores of
eternity. I heard the wail of these hosts until I found
myself resolved, whatever else I might do or not do,
to echo the sound of that ocean in the ears of
Christendom."*

A well-known essayist, in an exquisite vision of
human life, beheld an immense valley traversed by an
ever-rolling flood. A bridge of black and broken piers
stretched away into the boundless tide, and was lost
to view in the thick mist on the farther shore. Multitudes of people streamed to the fatal arches and sunk
in the abyss of waters. By a slight mental effort, we
can still gaze on that mystic river; for, deep and dark,
it flows sullenly and silently on to the ocean of
eternity. The inspired Psalmist beheld the generations of men, as they were swept noiselessly away
from the earth, and said, "Thou carriest them away
as with a flood." Beyond the mysterious bridge are
the thick clouds of a dark unknown, impalpable
except as revelation fringes them with the splendor
of an immortal hope. Millions of human beings
throng to the crumbling arch, sink into the flowing

---

* Joseph Cook, *Monday Lectures*, March 12, 1883.

tide, and are borne on to the changeless destinies of the future and the eternal.

Compute, if you can, as the endless procession passes on to the spirit world. Eight million of Jews, from almost every nation under heaven, a veil over their hearts, and still for the most part refusing to look to the 'pierced Saviour, lead the way. Nominal Christians from favored lands of Europe, scenes of Bible interest, and the natives of South America, stupefied and deluded by the corruptions and senseless mummeries of their religion, swell the helpless throng, and speed beyond the reach of any earthly ministry. Mussulmans from sections of three continents, the east of Europe, the north of Africa, and the west of Asia, such centres as Mecca, and Bagdad, and Aleppo, some of the best and fairest portions of the globe, follow the false prophet, and are enveloped in a smoke as that of the bottomless pit:

> "A saintly, murderous brood,
> To carnage and to Koran given,
> Who think through unbeliever's blood
> Lies their directest path to heaven."

Still others march past, only to vanish in darkness. There are the swarthy millions of Hindostan, bearing the symbols of their grotesque superstition, priest and pariah, thug and fakir, pilgrim and devotee, one hundred and sixty million of the worshippers of Brahma, blindly treading the pathway of mystery, and going down where the black billows close over them. The Saviour by His atonement has bridged the awful gulf, but they know nothing of that "new and living way." There is still a mightier multitude, at least four hundred millions, nearly a third of the human race, adherents of Buddha and Confucius, drifting on the shoreless ocean of the unseen and eternal; and, supposing that these teeming millions should pass you at the rate of one thousand an hour, night and day, more than forty-five years would be required to complete the dreary procession. But there is still another touching and pathetic appeal to Christian sympathy. Two hundred million of the sons and daughters of Africa, branded with the untold wrongs of ages, plead for pity and for help, and pass sorrowfully on to their destined and unknown future. Numerous tribes from yet unchristianized isles of the sea, and the roaming red races of our western forests and prairies follow in the rear, and hurry on to the land of silence and shade. What is to become of these untold millions? Where shall they spend their everlasting days? How, laden and polluted with sin and crime, can they find their way from the dark river to the gates of gold, or how enter the city of unsullied purity?

We rejoice in the thought, for which inspiration furnishes an abundant warrant, that, without respect of persons, every one of every nation that works out the righteousness of the dispensation under which he is placed, shall be accepted of God. "But the fearful, and unbelieving, and abominable, and murderers, and whoremongers, and sorcerers, and idolaters, and all liars, shall have their portion in the lake that burneth with fire and brimstone: which is the second death." And never should we forget that such depravities, as God unconditionally condemns, are characteristic of heathenism in every part of the world. O ye followers of the compassionate Redeemer, can you gaze unmoved upon scenes of guilt, weariness and woe? Is there not an irresistible impulse to some effort for the rescue of the perishing? Will you not care for the dying, tell them of God's pardoning love, and lead them to the fountain for sin and uncleanness? Hear you not the pleading voice, " Come over and help us?" There is a cry of souls longing for some deliverer. To each one comes the call. The obligation is of a personal character. Can any Christian man or woman turn away unmoved from the painful and piteous wail of suffering and sinful humanity? Salvation! O sound out the glad message to all the nations of the earth. Tell it out among the heathen, that a ransom has been found, and that they need not go down to the pit. But haste! Your mission is as that of one who bears a reprieve: hope to the despairing, and life to the dying.

To some extent the sense and significance of the Macedonian cry may have been realized, and rightly interpreted. But to know the heathen world, its awful and utter darkness and misery, and its need of the gospel, there must be a closer contact with Brahmanical and Buddhistic systems of idolatry and superstition, and with uncivilized and multitudinous races and tribes of Africa and isles of the sea.

"The vast old structure of the Veda religion, venerable by the suffrage of thirty centuries, upheld by tens of millions of the finest population in Asia, cherished by a pertinacity which has hitherto seemed immovable, adorned by temple after temple, celebrated in festivity after festivity, magnificent by processions and all public pomp, cemented by the indissoluble bonds of caste, and by a fixity of usage such as has never existed elsewhere."—*William Arthur.*

II.

CIVILIZED HEATHENISM: HINDUISM AND THE HINDUS.

HINDUISM is the central fortress of civilized heathenism. The world has no other such closely compacted system of error. It may be fairly regarded as the master-piece of the deceiver. Hoary with age, it challenges attention on the ground of its great antiquity. Its temples are magnificent, and its ritual adapted to the popular sense. Millions of priests avow their belief in countless millions of gods, and all are pledged to the perpetuation of this Brahmanical religion. Rising height above height, like the ranges and ridges of the Himalaya, the shadows of this stupendous and embattled structure seem to darken the day, and its proud spires to pierce the skies. Mysticisms and superstitions, penances and pilgrimages, transcendentalisms, adaptation to mental peculiarities, and penetrating grasp of the institutions and usages of national and social life, contribute to its moulding force, and combine to constitute it the mightiest of earth's idolatries. Hinduism numbers one hundred and sixty million of adherents. One of the most eminent of modern missionaries, when first confronted by this towering and frowning citadel of error, realized keenly the sense of his own weakness, and the utter insufficiency of human resource. A feeling came over him, such as he might have had if he had undertaken to cut down the primeval forest, with the blade of a knife, to level the Himalayas with a pickaxe, or to empty the Ganges with a teacup. "What field on the surface of the globe can be compared to Hindustan, stretching from the Indus to the Ganges, and from the Himalaya to Cape Comorin, in point of magnitude and accessibility combined, and peculiarity of claims on British Christians, the claims of not less than" two hundred millions "of fellow-subjects, sunk beneath the load of the most debasing superstitions, and the cruelest idolatries that ever polluted the surface of the earth, or brutalized the nature of man?"*

Between the earlier philosophy and the later and popular forms of Hinduism, there are numerous and bewildering differences, complex and contradictory aspects. The original Vedic idea of God seems to be that of an essence, analogous to space, self-existent and eternal. But the simple sublimity of primal conception soon begins to merge into pantheism, and passes on to the multiplied mythologies of polytheism. Unity diverges into numerous ramifications. The system is developed by the additions and accretions of ages. As the banyan of that land, its shoots are endlessly multiplied. "Like the sacred tree of India which from a single stem sends out innumerable

---

* Life of Dr. Duff, Vol. 1, p. 197.

branches destined to descend to the ground and become trees themselves, till the parent stock is lost in the dense forest of its own offshoots, so has this pantheistic creed rooted itself firmly in the Hindu mind, and spread its ramifications so luxuriantly that the simplicity of its root-dogma is lost in an exuberant growth of monstrous mythologies." *

A Hindu of the upper class believes that a self-existent principle may subsist under two modes. An essential condition, the point and perfection of felicity, consummation of bliss, is that of profound and utter quiescence and insensibility. But there was a period, a passing moment, when BRAHMAN roused up from the long deep stupor of ages, and exercised a potent and productive energy. Three gods, Brahma, Vishnu, and Siva, the Hindu trinity, constitute the divine manifestation of an eternal essence. Complexity of relation finds expression in a passage of Kalidasa—regarded by Professor Williams as "the greatest of Indian poets." Evidently there is a perpetual interchange of function:

"In these three Persons the one God was shewn—
Each first in place, each last—not one alone;
Of Siva, Vishnu, Brahma, each may be
First, second, third, among the blessed Three."

Brahma is regarded as creator. The material universe, according to the Hindu conception, is an emanation rather than an exercise of creative energy. It is an outflowing, like the light from the sun. "As the

---

* Hinduism, Prof. Monier Williams, p. 11.

threads from the spider, the tree from the seed, the fire from the coal, the stream from the fountain, the waves from the sea, so is the world produced out of Brahma." This deity of the Hindu temple and worship is usually represented as a figure of four faces. A philosophical formula, "I am Brahma, and he who knows that knows all," claims for him a reality of existence, in comparison with which everything in the visible universe must be looked upon as illusory and transient.

Vishnu, the second member of the triad, supposed to pervade and conserve all worlds, obtains homage as the preserver. This popular god is fabled to have had ten *incarnations*. May not these come yet to form the groundwork of belief in the Incarnate One, the Word that was made flesh and dwelt among us? The memory of Vishnu's actions, preserved and perpetuated in the sacred records, constitutes the most popular element in Hindu religious literature. In some temples the god may be seem in a form partly human, and in part resembling a fish; for, according to the legend, based doubtless on some tradition of the historic flood, he was incarnated as a fish to save the progenitor of the human race from an overflowing flood. Another incarnation is that of Krishna, "the dark god," represented in the form of a black idol; an appearance assumed for the destruction of Kansa, the representative principle of evil. Krishna is the most popular of Hindu deities; and, notwithstanding the distortion and exaggeration of this incarnation idea, as traced out in

Brahmanical legends, may we not hope that it shall yet be the means of preparing the minds of swarthy millions of eastern worshippers for the acceptance of Jesus Christ, the Saviour of the world?

Siva, the third member of the sacred triad, held to be the dissolver and destroyer of the universe, is regarded as the principal agent in the various changes that sweep on in a constant succession. This character is often depicted and shaped forth in hideous and repulsive forms. It is said that some of the images of the god are too abominable to be described. But a still fouler and more revolting form is that of his consort, the black goddess Kali; armed with sharp instruments, decorated by a necklace of skulls, clotted hair, and face and bosom smeared with blood. Kali is claimed as the presiding goddess of the infernal and terrible thugs; for whose honor and glory they murder their victims, and by whose energy their feet are made swift to shed blood. These be thy gods, O India!

To Hindu sacred *literature* an important place must be assigned.

The immense treasures of the Sanskrit, that "language of the gods," are being rapidly unsealed. At the foundation lies the three-fold Veda; mantra, brahmana, and upanishad: pure knowledge, imagined to have issued like breath from the Supreme. Vedic mantras, mainly metrical composition, are forms of prayer and praise. The rig-veda is the first and purest part of the mantra, and contains over a thousand hymns and rapturous ascriptions. It is regarded with profound reverence, said to shine in its own light, and to reveal absolute perfection; but, through rapt effusions, a declension from simple and primitive truth to pantheistic doctrine can be readily traced. Elements are personified. Powers of nature are identified with various divinities. Objects of religious adoration are multiplied. "God is everything, and everything is God."

The brahmanas, or second portion of the Veda, mostly of prose composition, expand and expound the merit of sacrifice, and develop and prescribe an elaborate and complicated system of priestly service. During the period of brahmana ascendency, every prominence was given to sacrificial offering. Numerous victims were immolated in almost every religious service, and the altars of the land perpetually streamed with blood.

To the upanishads, the third and last portion of the Veda, consisting of prose aphorisms and occasional verse, designed to unfold and illustrate the sacred doctrine of the mantras, Hinduism is mainly indebted for its mysticism and transcendentalism. Here may be found the source of a principal philosophical dogma, the transmigration of souls through a succession of bodies. And of all delusions, cunning inventions, or vain and foolish imaginations, that ever tortured the minds of poor, fallen humanity, the most dreary, oppressive, and painfully elaborated, is that of transmigration. Souls are regarded as an emanation from the eternal source, but doomed to a repeated succession of bodies, nearer or more distant from the fountain and fulness of perfection. They are held to be in perpetual transition; passing from body to body, from plant to plant, from animal to animal, from divinity to divinity, in sad and weary series and succession, without repose, destitute of joy, unable to arrest the stern monotony of change; treading, according to demerit or merit, the god's slowly-grinding mill; sinking into abysses of horror, or rising by gradual stages to an exalted felicity; dreaming of an ultimate absorption into the essential principle of the universe, the ideal of perfection, of endless and infinite bliss.

The real scriptures of the Hindu, however, as we are assured, because better known and perused, are the *puranas*. These are legendary histories, a voluminous and conglomerate collection of traditions and mythologies, measuring and marking an immense and deep distance and deterioration from the Vedic age. The original idea of the purana seems to have been an elucidation of matters belonging to some holy place, or the instruction of the people at great national festivals. There is no basis of fact or reason. They launch a system of cosmogony that shrivels before the light of science. Genealogies of the gods and unconnected traditions form a fabulous chronolgy. Time is of no account. Periods stretch back into the recesses of remote ages. Through a series of legendary narratives, resembling the coloring and Oriental extravagance of the *Arabian Nights' Entertainments*, these wonderful poems are brought down to the history and associations of the place to which they are dedicated.

It is affirmed that the history of mind in India corresponds to that of Europe. Every western system of thought, we are told, has had its counterpart in Asia. "Precisely the same topics which are brought to the front in religious discussions in the Occident, between Christianity and unbelief, are those which are at the front in the Orient."* As the product of rich and ripe Sanskrit scholarship, a superb series of Oxford translations, "The Sacred Books of the East," have been published for the benefit of English readers. The literature of that wonderful land, reaching back through a space of three thousand years, has been brought within the range of an ordinary student. The seal of mystery has been broken. It is evident, as thus represented, that Eastern speculations contain subtle philosophy, suggest ethical truth, and inculcate moral precept and social virtue. There is, at some points, a striking coincidence with what has claimed or come to be distinctively known as "modern thought." Occasional flashes indicate a rare intuition or insight into the profound necessities of the human soul. Under one guise or another, especially in the fabled incarnations, there are traces of traditional truth, and the idea of a needed Deliverer and Restorer. But thoughts that possess anything of religious or philosophic power and value are probably drift from some period of patriarchal revelation. With many acknowledged excellencies, and with great and abounding beauty and

---

* Joseph Cook, *Monday Lecture*, January 29th, 1883.

luxuriance of metaphor and style, these sacred books teem with worthless legends, monstrous credulities, the veriest puerilities, and the sheerest absurdities of the human imagination. Taken as a whole, with all their magnificence of expression, they are the darkness and not the light of Asia.

The literature of India, during thick mazes of the past, has been a source and secret of strength to Hinduism. But the deep night of ignorance is passing away; and in the future it may supply a potent instrument for the overthrow of an ancient and organized system of error. It contains history that facts disprove, and theories of the physical universe that science completely explodes. The Hindu student, as he comes to comprehend the leading principles of elementary knowledge, discovers the imposture and fabulous nature of writings which he once venerated as of indisputable authority. The spirit of inquiry thus awakened led to the conversion of Narayan Sheshadri, a gifted Brahman, to whose fervent and fluent utterances many of us have listened with delight. As he stood one day upon the beach at Bombay, swept into a foaming tempest by the fury of the monsoon, a sacred legend recurred to his mind. One of the mighty sages was said to have drunk up all the water of all the oceans of the earth. Was that story credible? A chill of doubt was experienced. Other extravagances of the shasters came under review. Faith was shaken. Inquiry failed to satisfy the understanding. From Brahmanism he turned to Christianity. The Bible was found and felt to be no cunningly devised fable.

Historic and scientific myths, when once disproved cannot be re-established. Incongruous elements in the Hindu system of doctrine and ritual are strangely and strikingly analogous to the mixture of iron and clay in the colossal image of Oriental vision: "Thou sawest till that a stone was cut out of the mountain without hands, which smote the image upon his feet that were of iron and clay, and broke them in pieces. Then was the iron, the clay, the brass, the silver, and the gold, broken to pieces together, and became like the chaff of the summer threshing floors; and the wind carried them away, that no place was found for them: and the stone that smote the image became a great mountain, and filled the whole earth."

Temples are a prominent feature of Hinduism. Benares alone boasts ten thousand splendid fanes. India is a land of superb and stately structures. The peerless Taj Mahal, or crown of edifices—a magnificent mausoleum at Agra—is said to have been "designed by Titans and finished by jewellers." The Seringham pagoda, near Trichinopoly, "an awful and indescribably vast fabric," was erected at a cost equal to that of St. Paul's. There are several groups of religious buildings in the Tanjore district, each one of which involved an expenditure equal to that of an English cathedral. Hindu temples, however, have little resemblance to the ecclesiastical edifices of Christendom. In architectural idea and outline, they seem to have more in common with the Hebrew temple at Jerusalem—court within court, terrace rising above terrace, and a diminished central site for the main sanctuary. The space occupied by a popular idol in India is usually flanked by extensive enclosures, comprising several acres. "As if in unconscious mockery of Divine revealings, the city of priests and prostitutes, which forms the Vaishnava or Savaite temples, lies four-square for a mile on each side, entered by imposing gateways, and dominated by towers of gigantic height. But as you pass through court after court to the hideous gloom of the contemptible sanctuary, and approach the obscene penetralia, the buildings diminish in size and elaboration."* In the vicinity of a famous idol, numerous and costly shrines are erected by wealthy natives, and such munificence is deemed to be exceedingly meritorious in its character.

But what shall be said of the idols, in a land that is wholly given to idolatry? In addition to more exalted divinities, the minor gods and goddesses are all but innumerable. A divine essence is supposed to permeate the visible universe, and the catalogue is being constantly enlarged. Heavenly bodies, various productions of the earth, beneficent rivers, the mysterious wind, the cloud-capped mountain, the spreading banyan, the sacred ox, the gamboling monkey, the noxious reptile, stocks and stones, mean and miscellaneous things, fair or foul, angel or demon, through hope or through fear, find a place in the pantheon. The Hindu makes to himself graven images, the likeness

---

* Life of Dr. Duff, Vol. II., p. 145.

of anything in heaven above, or in the earth beneath, or in the waters under the earth, and bows down to them and worships them.

Walls, towers, and gateways of temples, especially in the south of India, are sculptured with mythological groups. They exhibit infamous acts such as are ascribed to the gods, in whose honor the shrine has been dedicated. It has been said that if in the midst of their quarrels and treacheries, obscenities and atrocities, "the gods of the Hindu heaven had been suddenly overtaken by a statuary death," these abominable sculptures might be the agglomeration of them all. No man who has once seen the gates can ever forget them. It is a strange and hideous sight. "And then to see groups of children playing before this pile of sculptured temptation, looking at it, gazing on it, regarding it as the shrine and embodiment of religion. It brings a feeling of oppressive sickness. You feel as if Milton's Belial, the dissolutest spirit that fell, were standing by and pointing to that as the audacious monument of a victory he won over everything pure in man." *

India is the land of pilgrimages. It has numerous cities and shrines and streams of reputed sanctity; and for the sake of penance, ablution, or some ceremonial observance, multitudes of people are perpetually on the move. At the great annual festivals, in honor of popular idols, thousands of pilgrims throng

---

* Arthur's *Mission to the Mysore*, *Methodist Magazine*, 1846, p. 584.

to the temple service. Many of these are weary wanderers after rest. Waters of sacred rivers are regarded as efficacious for the cleansing of moral pollution; and, as the most magnificent river, the Ganges is thought to be specially and signally potent for the purification of the soul. As a means of salvation, or for the accumulation of merit, a Hindu achieves immense feats of devotion. Think of a pilgrim starting from the source of the Ganges, traversing the river to its mouth, measuring the same distance on the opposite bank, and getting back to the starting-point at the end of six years! But what can protracted penance avail? "Thou desirest not sacrifice, else would I give it."

Sacrificial offerings are prescribed in the brahmanas, and amongst some tribes human sacrifices are still deemed efficacious and meritorious. An American missionary furnishes a vivid description of a sanguinary scene which he witnessed, and of its surroundings. The ceremony was performed in the night. A hurried booth had been constructed for the idol. Solitary lights threw deeper shadows into the background. The god was garlanded with flowers. Sacred ashes were supplied to the devotees, for the purpose of rubbing their heads and bodies. Strange noises, through the trilling of the tongue, were made by the women of the crowd. Fowls and sheep were slain. The offerers of the sacrifices, bearing their bleeding and quivering victims, hurried out into the darkness of the night. No wonder there was a deepened desire to make known to those dark idolaters the efficacy of the one great Sacrifice, and to point them to Him who is "the propitiation for our sins: and not for ours only, but also for the sins of the whole world."

The spirit of Brahmanism is hard and cruel in the extreme. Until disallowed by Government, its dire precepts were remorselessly inculcated, and no act was considered more acceptable to the gods than that of voluntary suffering. Torture is deemed meritorious in proportion to its intensity. In former times, a woman that offered herself for the funeral pile, on the death of her husband, won a bright record. When Christianity commenced its beneficent mission in India; ten thousand widows were annually burnt to death. The eminent Serampore missionary, Dr. Carey, on attempting an organized movement for the abolition of the suttee, found that within a circle of thirty miles around Calcutta, during a period of three months there had been no less than three hundred such immolations. Mothers worshipped the goddess of murder, and, under the influence of dread superstition, laid their hapless infants on the bleeding altars of their superstition. Aged and helpless parents were carried to the banks of some sacred river, and left there to die. By wildly prostrating themselves beneath the wheels of the ponderous car of Juggernaut, multitudes committed suicide. Mangled bodies were supposed to appease the dread divinities. We still remember the missionary appeal:

> "Light on the Hindu shed,
>   The maddening idol train!
> The flame of the suttee is dire and red,
>   And the fakir faints with pain;
> The dying moan on their cheerless bed,
>   By the Ganges laved in vain."

But, mainly as the result of public opinion, created by Christian missionaries, a great and growing change has been effected. Suttee fires have been extinguished. Infanticide has been abolished. The madness of prostration beneath the cruel and crushing wheels of an idol-car is prohibited. Hindu gods wait in vain for their prescribed libations of blood. Dark and horrible practices, "which the edicts and energies of such emperors as Akbar and Aurungzebe could not restrain, tremble before the cross of Christ." Facts such as these, well brought out in "the Land of the Veda," mark the progress of the mission movement in Hindustan, and the beneficent changes that are passing over the people of that great country.

Caste is a distinctive and enormous feature and wrong of the Hindu system. This pernicious law, in all probability, had its origin in social inequalities. Between the proud Aryan conqueror and the despised aborigines of the soil, at the formative period of Brahmanism, there must have been a broad barrier of social grade. Religion, instead of bridging the extremes, dug a deep trench. A great gulf was fixed. "Now the Indian system of caste is simply a vast and prolonged attempt to substitute artificial for natural distinctions, to create and perpetuate hard and fast lines of separation between the various orders of society, and the occupations, privileges, dignities, pertaining to them. It caught society at a point where historical causes had led to certain social divisions of rank and occupation, and it petrified these divisions for all coming time."* Through the operation of caste the Hindu people are distributed into separate classes, and must remain distinct from birth to death. The presumptuous pride of the priest, and the utter hopelessnsss of the pariah, are alike intensified and stereotyped by the force and fixity of immemorial usage. There cannot be alleviations or release. This iron law forms an essential part of the Brahmanical system, and may be regarded as the real test of Hinduism. Religion ought to be a cementing principle and a bond of union between man and man. But here it produces alienation, and operates as an engine of despotism. The tyranny of this law tells with terrible effect upon the social life of the people. A man of high rank may lose caste, and then the place that knew him can know him no more.

But the outcasts of India are most to be pitied. In many districts of the country, until recently, they were an excluded people; not permitted to reside in the city, to mingle with the crowd in the street, to listen to the reading of sacred books, or even to ask for charity at the street doors. There has been a slow and slight relaxation of former stringency, and the

---

* Dr. Caird, *Oriental Religions*, Humb. Lib., p. 11.

pariah is permitted to reside in an inferior corner of the town or village. But think of the degradation! An outcast cannot come into contact with more favored mortals of his own race and kindred. There is a thought continually forced upon him, that his touch is pollution, and that his presence is intolerable. Some hateful thing makes him an object of loathing and contempt. This man, created of God, redeemed by the precious blood of Christ, endowed with exalted moral and spiritual capabilities, and destined to immortality, is made to feel a sense of immeasurable humiliation. And even this baseness of condition does not exhaust the sum of his misery. Degradation must be transmitted to his children, and to his children's children. As far as he knows, there is no power in heaven or earth to release him from the curse, or to arrest the entail of sorrow and woe. Shall the Macedonian cry of the Hindu outcasts be unheeded? Through untold miseries,

"They call us to deliver
Their land from error's chain."

The ramification of such an institution can be easily imagined. Masses are held together by a chain, the links of which it has taken ages to forge and rivet. Every man is bound by the law of universal cohesion. A Hindu, unless he wrench himself from all the ties of national and social life, *can only move as his caste moves*. In this fact may be found a serious obstruction to the prosecution of Christian work in India. "What will become of my caste?" "Will not the proposed step endanger my caste?" "Are not the missionaries resolved to break up my caste?" These burning questions are inevitably forced to the front. At every point the subject touches Hindu thought and probes it to its very heart. But this adhesiveness of the social structure has an aspect of hopefulness. Even the severance of a single individual causes a jar through the complete fabric, and the impact of multiplied conversions must be productive of far-reaching results. If the pretensions of caste could be tolerated, the Brahman allowed to take supreme position, and inferior grades maintained, converts to Christianity would be rapidly increased, and the statistics of missions run into new and larger columns. But the Church of Christ cannot recognize any law of caste. "There is neither Jew nor Greek, there is neither bond nor free, there is neither male nor female: for ye are all one in Christ." There must be no compromise. Brahman and Sudra have to bow before the same altar, and to meet at the one communion.

"The chain of caste is broken," exclaimed the first of Carey's converts, "and who shall mend it?" Two years later a Brahman surrendered his sacred thread, and another link was severed. The scheme has been devised with subtle and infernal ingenuity; but, through the touch of spiritual power, and the influence of a Christian civilization, fetters shall fall away, and the hardness of steel be dissolved.

Indirect agencies have done a good work in India. Opportunities afforded by the last famine were signalized by noble deeds of kindness. Hinduism was placed in manifest and humiliating contrast to the Christian religion. Brahmans were consulted in the dire extremity. Wealth was lavished at the shrines of heathen gods. Ceremonial rites were scrupulously observed. Heathen help was fervently implored. But ritualistic service was all in vain. The heavens were as brass. Priests were impotent men. There was none to heed the suppliant's cry. In that hour of sore need, Christianity, as an angel of love and pity, moved through the land, and ministered to the sufferers.

A movement for the education of the women of India tends to social revolution. It has long been the battle-ground of evangelistic enterprise. The avowal of such a purpose, in direct opposition to the beliefs and habits of ages, had to encounter an excited and indignant feeling. But missionary intrepidity was not to be shaken. A marked and manifest change has recently found expression in public and popular opinion and sentiment. Solid ramparts of superstition and prejudice have been fairly pierced. An immense impetus has been given to social progress. Bound up with this organized effort are the hopes and happiness of untold and unborn millions. One of the most thrilling of Oriental stories is that of Rama rescuing his beautiful bride from the clutches of Ravannah, the demon-king. Hanuman, the son of the wind, discovered her prison-house, and gave assurance of deliverance. At the suggestion of Hanuman, Rama drew a bow, and sent it to the monster's heart. The power of darkness was destroyed. Sita, the princess, was led forth from captivity to share her husband's throne. A warfare has been commenced for the rescue of the sorrowful zenana captive. Dungeon walls are thickly beleaguered. Sharp are the arrows from the polished quiver of the mighty archer. Demons of superstition are surely doomed. India's beautiful daughter, rescued from a long and foul imprisonment, shall be brought into the light and blessedness of a new and purer life. Redeemed by Christ Jesus, robed in righteousness, the ransomed one shall share in coronation splendour and triumph: "She shall be brought to the king in raiment of needlework: the virgins, her companions that follow her, shall be brought unto thee. With gladness and rejoicing shall she be brought: they shall enter into the king's palace."

An extraordinary intellectual movement also ranks among the signs of the times in India. Keshub Chunder Sen and other cultured and non-Christian Hindus are leaders of the new faith. A general sanction is given to revealed truth, and recognition is freely accorded to the labors of missionaries. Idolatry is renounced, and caste rejected. Hope has long been cherished that this uprising of mind would receive a spiritual baptism, and be brought under the influence of Christianity. "Our hearts are touched," said Chunder Sen, a splendid rhetorician, "conquered, overcome by a higher power; and that power is Christ: Christ, not the British Government, rules India! None but Christ deserves the precious diadem of the Indian crown, and he shall have it." But, notwithstanding such brilliant and impassioned utterances, it is apparent that the reformation has run to the extreme of rationalism. A hymn of the "new dispensation" crystallizes characteristic tenets: "Many a Yogi and Rishi, many a saint and devotee, have dispensed the true religion. Ancient teachers, the great leaders of mind and moulders of thought, Shiva and Shuka, Chitanya, whose soul was the storehouse of God's love, Muni and Moses, Jesus and Mohammed, form one holy family of saints. All these are honored, the objects of deepest reverence. But no one can stand in the place of God, as a mediator or incarnation." Brahmoism has been called a Christianity without Christ. As represented by the Somaj, or by the new dispensation, it cannot be a regenerative power for India.

One of the saddest thoughts in connection with the present intellectual ferment of the Hindu mind, is the drift towards a dark and dreary sea of unbelief. Old creeds are being undermined. Structures of an immense antiquity are in the process of upheaval. But many advanced students, in the abandonment of their ancestral religion, fail to reach the solid ground of evangelical belief. Rationalism is the natural and legitimate outcome of a purely secular education. From the complete course of Government instruction, up to the present time, there has been a rigid exclusion of the distinctive teachings of revealed truth. There is nothing in the pages of Bain or Mill, or of any text-book of Western science, to guide a perplexed and eager inquirer to him who is "the way, and the truth, and the life." A syllogism cannot resolve the problem of sin or of salvation. Teachers are not permitted to encourage the idea that Christianity must supplant Hinduism, that Christ Jesus should be preferred to Krishna, or that "the blood of sprinkling" is more efficacious for moral and spiritual cleansing than the waters of the Ganges. "Launched out," says a recently returned missionary, "on a shoreless sea of speculation, cut clean from the old mooring, sent adrift o'er a perilous ocean of bewilderment, with no surer guide than scientific text-books, the present state of some will warrant the assertion that but a few years will see the rocks of downright infidelity strewn with the shattered and battered wrecks of some of India's finest and noblest sons."

The Hindu mind is in transition. Fears have been expressed as to the result. But there is good reason to believe that the movement is in the direction of a purer faith. Missions are not to be measured by mere statistics. Progress is not limited to the facts of individual conversion. Idolatries of Eastern cities and sacred centres are buttressed and fortressed on every side. Seams and rents, produced by undermining operations, can scarcely be expected to reveal soon or suddenly the crumbling weakness of such a structure. It may be that the faith and patience of missionaries, and of people by whom the enterprise is sustained, shall be yet more sorely tested. But there cannot be a doubt as to the future and final result. A wedge, that ensures ultimate dissolution, has been inserted into the compact mass of error and superstition. Christianity is piercing the Brahmanical system to its very heart. Many are beginning to realize the folly and futility of idol worship. Heathen hearts are yearning for an unknown good. Evangelistic work is being promoted by a hundred unconscious and unconnected agencies. Processes of which no immediate account can be taken are everywhere in active and vigorous operation. A thousand avenues are being cleared for the entrance of new and ameliorating ideas and elements. Two million of boys, the men of the future, receive instruction in secular and mission schools. "The Hindu mind," says the historian of the nineteenth century, "is awaking from the sleep of ages." It is the belief of Sir Charles Trevelyan that "when the absorption of truth has gone far enough, native opinion will declare itself, and a nation be born in a day." Every other faith, according to the competent testimony of Sir Herbert Edwards, is decaying, and "Christianity alone is beginning to run its course." "The time is not far distant," spoke a Brahman to a Jatrapore missionary, "when your religion will be our religion, and your God our God. *It must come to that.*"

A testimony of exceptional value, in regard to this subject of transition, may be given at greater length. The Right Hon. W. E. Baxter, M.P., since a recent visit to India, has given some impressions of what he witnessed. From the sacred city of Benares, in the

Maharajah's state barge, he slowly glided down the Ganges. The scene could never be forgotten. It was in the early morning. "The sun had just risen, and its first rays were tinging the tops of domes and towers, temples and palaces. Thousands of worshippers in bright garments were on the steps leading down to the sacred streams, while the voices of fakirs, and the tinkling of cymbals filled the air. Never had he beheld anything more picturesquely beautiful; but this city, like the Athens of the Apostle, was wholly given to idolatry. Not altogether wholly! One of the missionaries deplored the slow progress of the mission. There were, however, five hundred boys in its schools; the number of pilgrims was falling off; the temples were getting into debt; and, year by year, as the sapping and mining process went on all over India there was greater liberty experienced in the proclamation of Christian truth. Colleges and institutions throughout the country, from Lahore to Calcutta, admirably conducted, were crowded with intelligent youth, learning the literature and science and religion of Europe, who would one day become the lights of Asia. It would be difficult to exaggerate the influence which these seminaries in the end would exert; they might bring about a great social revolution even before the end of the century." *

The Gospel of Christ is the hope of India. The Macedonian cry of its teeming millions can only be

---

* *Sunday at Home*, Nov. 1882, p. 751.

met and stayed by the proclamation of a glad evangel: "The blood of Jesus Christ his Son cleanseth us from all sin." Missionaries that have lived and labored the longest beneath that burning sky avow an unbounded faith in their appointed message. The proud priests of Brahma can only regard the doctrine of the cross with disdain. Occasionally they halt on the outskirts of a listening crowd, in one of the sacred cities where Hinduism still towers in its strength. Brahmanical pretensions are denounced, and the fall of the system predicted. Dark eyes flash with anger. But the appliances of the preacher, as he points the multitude to "the Lamb of God which taketh away the sin of the world," seem to be so unutterably feeble for the work attempted, and the apparent impression on the minds of the mass of the people so very slight, that an expression of bitterness and hate may be seen to change to something more of cool and ineffable contempt and scorn.

Yet India has already many witnesses for Jesus. Conspicuous cases of individual conversion, even in the citadel centres of the north, contain the pledge and promise of a future work of God. Redeeming love melts away the encrustations of spiritual pride. Through the sweetness and power of saving grace, the hardness of prejudice is dissolved. Indifference gives place to a tender and inexpressible interest in sacred themes. The subtile controversialist is transformed into a true and loving disciple of the Lord Jesus Christ. Even the countenance of a genuine convert tells of an unutterable emotion. There is the gladness of transition from darkness to light, from doubt to faith and genuine peace. Calcutta needs exactly the same gospel as that which St. Paul preached in the proud city of Corinth: "But we preach Christ crucified, unto the Jews a stumbling-block, and unto the Greeks foolishness; but unto them which are called, both Jews and Greeks, Christ the power of God, and the wisdom of God. Because the foolishness of God is wiser than men; and the weakness of God stronger than men." *

---

* Hinduism, however, is not the only factor in the problem of India's evangelization. Fifty millions of people in that land are followers of the false prophet. The spirit of Mohammedanism has been embittered by the failure of cherished schemes of conquest. Ambition burns to found Moslem empire, and to bring back the proud days and dynasty of the Delhi emperors. To the messenger of the cross, adherents of the Koran are less accessible than the idolaters around them. This is scarcely a matter of surprise. Everything connected with Christianity is intimately identified with the name and nationality of the conqueror. The bare idea of submission wounds the pride, revives a sense of humiliation, and excites a feeling of derision and hate.

"Rising near the base of the Himalayas and spreading over half the continent of Asia, and extending to the more populous of the adjacent islands, Buddhism everywhere takes the tinge of the soil over which it flows, and the complexion of its adherents is not more diverse than the aspects which it presents in Thibet and Tartary, Ceylon and Burmah, China and Japan."—*Dr. W. A. P. Martin.*

III.

CIVILIZED HEATHENISM: BUDDHISM AND THE BUDDHISTS.

AN immense tableland stretches over the vast expanse of Central Asia. The plateau of Thibet, forming the highest part of this elevation, is traversed by a stupendous mountain ridge, known by the natives as "the roof of the world." If from the icy heights of Pamir, the crowning summit of this ridge, as from another Pisgah, our vision could sweep the continent, we should look down upon the most populous lands of the globe. To the north there are the extensive and almost unexplored territories of Mongolia and Tartary. On the south, the snow-clad peaks of the Himalayas pierce the skies, and the roots of everlasting hills strike down into the glowing and densely-populated plains of Hindustan. Races and regions of Afghanistan, Persia, and Asiatic Turkey are to the west; and, in the direction of the rising sun, beyond the rocks of Thibet, the almost boundless empire of China stretches away to distant wall and sea. Through the greater part of this vast range, in some of its forms, Buddhism is the prevailing religion. "This great faith of Asia, in the number of its followers and the area of its prevalence, surpasses any other form or creed. Four hundred millions of our race live and die in the tenets of Gautama; and the spiritual dominions of this ancient teacher extend, at the present time, from Nepaul and Ceylon, over the whole Eastern peninsula, to China, Japan, Thibet, Central Asia, Siberia, and Swedish Lapland. India itself might fairly be included in this magnificent empire of belief; for though the profession of Buddhism has for the most part passed away from the land of its birth, the mark of Gautama's sublime teaching is stamped ineffaceably upon modern Brahmanism. Forests of flowers are daily laid upon stainless shrines, and countless millions of lips daily repeat the formula, *I take refuge in Buddha.*" *

Millions of Asiatics hear of no Saviour but the Sakya-muní. To them, according to highest priestly ideal, he is the joy and gladness of the whole world. Helpless ones are encouraged to look to him as the only helper. He is said to be "the dewa of the dewas, and the brahma of the brahmas." Though great and powerful, yet he is kind and compassionate. Rich gifts are believed to be in store for the suppliant who only softly pronounces the name of the illustrious Sage, or that, in obedience to sacred inculcation, gives a few grains of rice for charity. But what can highest human strength and resource avail for the salvation of a sinful race? O, for the revelation of Him in whom "dwelleth the fulness of the Godhead bodily!"

---

* *The Light of Asia*, Preface.

The founder of this Eastern faith, Gautama or "Saddartha styled on earth," according to tradition, was the son of Suddhodana, a rajah that ruled at Kapilavastu in the north of India. Because of tribal pre-eminence, he had the surname of Sakya-muni; and, consequent upon the promulgation of his creed, he came to be known as Buddha, the Sage or Enlightener. Like most Oriental princes, during early life, he had ample means for sensual gratification. But suddenly the pleasures, immunities, and privileges of rank and riches were renounced. He retired to a solitude. The fact of human depravity and misery became the subject of profound and prayerful thought. After a signal victory over the powers of darkness, according to legends of his life, and the fiercest assaults of pride and passion, Gautama obtained an extraordinary degree of illumination, and entered upon a kind of sublime and ethereal existence. He gave himself up to meditation, and to absorbing thought. A new scheme of morality and religion was evolved and formulated. Leading principles were enunciated in his first sermon: right views and high aims, kindly and upright behaviour, a harmless livelihood, perseverance in well-doing, intellectual activity and earnest thought.

Many of Buddha's maxims are admirable. They gleam with the light of a traditional truth, widely disseminated through that part of the world. But the teachings of Gautama ignore the fact of sin, and the exceeding sinfulness of sin; and to understand their impotence, as a means of regeneration, we must look deeper to the heart of the system. The words of this teacher are not spirit or life. They constitute a system of philosophy rather than a creed and standard of spiritual worship. Buddhism was proposed as a reform of Brahmanism. Extremes meet. Brahmanism is said to be faith without knowlege, a God without morality; and Buddhism is characterized as "knowledge without faith" and "morality without God."

There is a prevalent metaphysical notion in the East that the visible and material universe is but a transient manifestation of the Supreme Essence; that the human soul is an emanation from the eternal Spirit; that at some stage of existence, after successive transmigrations and innumerable miseries and vexations, the loftiest ideal of life shall be attained; that released from individual existence, there shall be an ultimate union with the essential principle of the universe:

> "Yon cloud which floats in heaven, the prince replied,
> Wreathed like gold around your Indra's throne,
> Rose thither from the tempest-driven sea;
> But it must fall again in tearful drops,
> Trickling through rough and painful water-ways,
> By cleft and nullah and muddy flood,
> To Gunga and the sea, wherefrom it sprang.
> Know'st thou, my brother, if be not thus,
> After their many pains, with the saints in bliss?" *

---

* *The Light of Asia*, Lib. Mag., Vol. 3rd, p. 280.

This central idea of Oriental philosophy, from the force of reaction, seems to have furnished the germ of Buddha's doctrinal scheme. Earnestly the Sage looked for deliverance from mundane and mortal miseries. Some alleviation there was in the accepted belief of the transmigration of souls. But there was a current theory that even the multitude of gods could not obtain exemption from the pain and uncertainties of change. It was understood that, at the will of the Supreme, the most exalted divinities were liable to alternate and successive periods of creation and absorption. The creature is subject to bondage. Aggregate of action in previous states and stages of existence, for which there may have been little or no responsibility, determines the nature of subsequent birth and life. The insect, that perishes at the close of the summer noon, may enshrine the soul of a former inhabitant of earth. Humanity may be reborn as a radiant angel, or the reverse of such process may be the result of transmigration. This consideration drove Gautama to sheer atheism, and led him to deny Supreme existence. There was no such Being in the universe. A new theory was propounded. "Existence is suffering." "Human passion is the cause of existence." But, through obedience to the laws of life, "the destruction of human passion may be obtained;" and, "by the extinction of passion, existence may be brought to an end." Means and methods are minutely prescribed to facilitate the process. Austerities and ceremonies are appointed, and the mortification of self is rigidly enforced. Retirement from the world, somewhat after the manner of mediæval monasticism, finds abundant encouragement, and is deemed to be exceedingly helpful to a saintly life. Immunities of the flesh are to be subdued, and vile necessities of appetite and passion strangled and slain. Each lust of the soul, as well as of the body, must be thoroughly mortified. The mind should be urged to abstraction. Nature will then yield up her deepest secrets. Through severity of self-abnegation the blessedness of *Nirvana* shall be attained.

To make sure that man in this world shall not reappear, under any new form of illusion and misery, the very elements of spiritual existence are to be extinguished. Personality must be utterly destroyed. Every root and tendril of desire and affection connected with the idea and anticipation of perpetuated and conscious life have to be sternly extirpated and severed from the soul. Meditation and absolute abstraction of thought and feeling are the gateways and avenues through which the Buddhist attains to the ultimate and coveted unity and rest; the fulness and felicity, as he dreams, of perfect and complete unconsciousness, a blessedness without emotion, thought, or sense. That creed makes it better not to be. The follower of Buddha is taught to aim at rest—a lifeless, nameless, sinless, stirless rest; a change that can know no change. To make sure of the devoutly-wished-for consummation, the process must begin here, and the mind be elevated to the level of a law under which impulse and desire shall be utterly repressed. Completeness of renunciation leads to the desired goal. Everything of earthly passion and purpose is forever extinguished. The life of man, according to a favourite simile, resembles an Indian lamp. "As flame cannot exist without oil, so individual existence depends on the cleaving to low and earthly things. If there is no oil in the lamp it will go out." *

But what is the Nirvana of this philosophical scheme? What shall be the *finale* or ultimate condition of the soul—trance or nihilism, absorption or extinction? Shall life be exhaled like the dew from the lotus leaf at sunrise, or absorbed as the rain-drop that "slips away into the shining sea?" Must consciousness fade out in the same manner as the flickering flame of a lamp that can never be re-lighted? The word "nirvana," according to various exponents of the Buddhist doctrine, may be understood to mean "without blowing," an eternal quiescence, "a state of calm which no breath of wind disturbs;" or it may mean "blowing out," as the extinguishing of a light, the complete extinction of being. Dr. Caird does not hesitate to pronounce that "this heaven of the Buddhists contains in it, at least explicitly, no positive element such as we express by the words moral and spiritual perfection, but is neither more nor less than absolute annihilation." †

---

* *Buddhism*, Rhys Davis, p. 114.
† *Oriental Religions*, Humbolt Lib., p. 24.

Such is pure Buddhism! It recognizes no Divine Personality, and it leaves man without God and without hope in the world. Personality would be regarded as a defect. Deity is an abstraction. Heart and flesh cry out in vain for the living God. Prayer is useless, and the idea of propitiation a delusion. Humanity is orphaned and desolate. There is no ear to hear, no heart to sympathize, no arm to save. Weakness cannot take hold upon strength. Lips of supplication are sealed. The heavens are as brass. Gautama "chokes the cry" of the helpless human soul. The more thoroughly a disciple or devotee of this much-vaunted system accepts its teachings and theories, the farther does he drift away from the idea of a living, personal God, and from the consolation and strength of a Divine Fatherhood.*

Sutras abound with generous phrases. The scheme of Sakya-muni extols brotherhood and charity, beneficence and almsgiving; but, in practical life, all these exhortations are neutralized. The spirit of the system, notwithstanding the glow of beautiful precept, tends to utter and intense selfishness. It isolates man from society. Abstraction is urged, and tender impulses are extinguished. Transcendental idealism and the life of a monk or hermit are incompatible with the deeds and demands of an active and practical philanthropy.

Buddhism, at its best, is not only atheistic and selfish

---

* "Buddha recognizes no supreme deity; the only God, he affirmed, is what man himself can become."—*Hinduism*, Monier Williams, p. 176.

in its teachings and tendencies, but its votaries are destitute of any inspiring and ennobling hope. In regard to the great questions of human origin and destiny, it is a sunless, starless, rayless religion. Its much-lauded nirvana is a mere vagary, a poetical idea, a beautiful dream, and can never arch the stormy sky of human life with the magnificent bow of an immortal hope. What a contrast to the fulness of joy, the home of the many mansions, the companionship of angels and glorified saints, the blessedness of the beatific vision, the rapture of endless praise, and the perpetuity of bliss, which Christianity reveals! Buddhism glories in the extinction of personality and of every capacity for eternal life. But, through the light and spiritual power of a nobler and purer revelation and religion, transcending the speculations of the Sakyamuni, an eminent Oriental saint exulted in hope: "For I know that my Redeemer liveth, and that he shall stand at the latter day upon the earth: and though after my skin worms destroy this body, yet in my flesh shall I see God: whom I shall see for myself, and mine eyes shall behold, and not another."

The Buddhist reformation began in the holy city of Benares, Northern India, about five centuries before the Christian era. Gautama was an enthusiastic and intrepid missionary, and his tenets were promulgated with a zeal and success that have never been exhibited or achieved by the emissaries of any other heathen religion. The new faith conquered the Himalayan countries, took possession of Ceylon, and penetrated to

Thibet, the empire of China, and the islands of Japan. Through contact or amalgamation with other Asiatic and idolatrous systems and religions, Buddhism has been greatly modified. An attempt has been made to define the doctrines of the Eastern Sage; but, in modern and prevalent Buddhism, there is very much that its philosophic founder would fail to recognize, and more that he would probably refuse to acknowledge. "Having been adopted by very savage and very civilized people—the wild hordes on the cold table-lands of Nepaul, Tartary and Thibet; the cultured Chinese and Japanese in their varying climes; and the quiet Sinhalese and Siamese, under the palm groves of the south—it has been so modified by the national characteristics of its converts, that it has developed into strangely inconsistent and even antagonistic beliefs."*

The purest type of Buddhism is now to be found in Ceylon. That island is regarded as the holy land of Asia. Thrice it was visited by Buddha in person. There his discourses were first committed to writing. The central mountain peak of that island, it is affirmed, still bears the impress of the Sage's foot. Nowhere else, in our time, has heathenism exhibited so much of vitality and of the spirit of aggressiveness. A keen controversy has for many years been carried on between Buddhist priests and Christian missionaries. An early incident of the dispute, as narrated by Spence Hardy, shows the temper of Buddha's champions, and

---

* *Buddhism*, Rhys Davis, p. 7.

the ease and effectiveness with which they wield their polished weapons. In connection with one of the great heathen festivals, a number of slips were printed at the mission press, and distributed among the pilgrims on their way to the chief temple. The first of these leaflets announced "Important information," and contained an emphatic passage: "We know that an idol is nothing in the world, and that there is none other God but one." An immediate reply was produced. The rejoinder was affixed to a tree, near one of the main thoroughfares, where it was read by thousands. "We know," was the retort, "that there is *no god* who is the giver of all good, and who lives for ever, existing in time past, present, and to come; and that none but Buddha is the creator and the donor of all sorrow-destroying tranquility." A second publication in the missionary series was headed "Good news," and contained an epitome of the whole gospel: "For God so loved the world, that he gave his only begotten Son, that whosoever believeth in him should not perish, but have everlasting life." The counterpart of this announcement was to the effect that another glorious incarnation appealed to the faith and gratitude of the people: "The present Buddha so much, so infinitely pitied Maraya, and all beings in every world, that resolving to become Buddha, he came down from heaven; though, on approaching the seat of Buddhaship, his design was opposed by the Dewa Maraya and his host; yet, having conquered and put him to flight, he became supreme Buddha, in order that all that believe him should not perish but obtain the happiness of nirvana." The third missionary declaration was entitled, "Divine instruction." It affirmed that "there is one God, and one mediator between God and man, the man Christ Jesus." An answer found equal publicity: "He who delights in the glorious sermons of the all-wise Buddha, more divine than the gods, who receives no false doctrine, and who perseveres in the performance of the meritorious actions, shall obtain divine and human enjoyments, with all other eternal blessings." Discussions in Ceylon have been marked by eminent ability. Men of literary and scholarly distinction have contended skilfully for the Christian faith, but among the champions of the heathen creed they have found foemen worthy of their steel.*

A special prominence, for good reason, has been assigned to these facts of the Buddhist controversy. Ceylon is the consecrated centre of this religious system, and the ground on which it can be studied to the best advantage. Throughout Central Asia there is a current tradition that from the holy island great changes are to be introduced into the popular faith. Whatever happens at that sacred spot makes its influence felt in every part of the Buddhist world. It would be impossible for us not to feel a thrill of interest in any of those movements that touch the hopes

---

* A native Wesleyan missionary, Rev. David de Silva, "well read both in Pali and Sanskrit," was the representative of Christianity in the latest public Buddhist controversy, in Ceylon, 1873.

or fears and mould the lives of so many millions of our fellowmen.

Buddhism has been a perpetual blight and no blessing to Ceylon. For ages it has been the dominant faith. There has been ample time for the fullest experiment. No region could be more favourable or fitting for its development. It signally adapts itself to each surrounding scene. Floral offerings are the special demand for Gautama's service of worship; and in this island everlasting spring abides. Flowers are in constant bloom. Ceylon is "the resplendent," the fairest "gem of the Indian Ocean," and "the brightest pearl on the brow of India." From central peak to the border of its snow-white coral, the land is pencilled in lines of soft and exquisite beauty. Language fails to depict the charm and fascination of scenery and climate. In the midst of mingled grandeur and loveliness, perfumed by the fragrance of cinnamon groves, Buddhism has erected its stately temples. Through gorgeous grounds, avenues of palms and other tropical foliage, the worshippers pass into the spacious sanctuaries of idolatry. Yellow-robed priests chant the doctrines of their national creed. But metaphysical subtleties are not comprehended by the mass of the people; and even moral inculcations have but little practical influence upon their hearts or lives. Men and women place bright garlands upon the altar, and bow before images of hard and hideous form and feature. There is no power to regenerate and save. A stanza of Heber's hymn, written in the early days of missionary enterprise, still tells the sad story:—

"What though the spicy breezes
 Blow soft o'er Ceylon's isle;
Though every prospect pleases,
 And only man is vile;
In vain, with lavish kindness,
 The gifts of God are strewn;
The heathen in his blindness
 Bows down to wood and stone."

Buddhism is the dominant religion of the large territory known as Cochin China. This peninsula, situated between China and India, and influenced by the civil and religious movements of both empires, with a numerous and mixed population, forms an important mission field. The great Baptist missionary, Judson, entered Burmah in 1813. Seven years he and his companions toiled in Rangoon before a single convert cheered their hearts or blessed their work. In this land the Buddhistic system is at its worst. But the faith and intrepidity of the great pioneer were never shaken. Three years after the commencement of the mission, signs of impatience began to be manifested by the people at home. "If they ask," he wrote, "what prospect of ultimate success is there? tell them, as much as there is in an almighty and faithful God, who will perform his promise, and no more." The work was heroically begun, and it has been nobly sustained, crowned with a magnificent success.

The kingdom of Siam is pre-eminently a stronghold of Buddhism. Beyond the rest of Asia it is distinguished for splendid temples and gigantic statues. Stupendous superstition obtains an undisputed supremacy over national feeling and sentiment. From palace to hovel the same religion prevails. The king, before his coronation, must don the yellow robe; and the bridegroom, before receiving his bride, must wear the same symbol. All associations and relationships of life are penetrated, pervaded, and shadowed, by the rites and requirements of this idolatrous and degrading system.

Buddhism has conquered the rocky region in the centre of the Asiatic continent. The mountains of Tibet abound with temples, monasteries, and other religious institutions. It is said that not less than eighty thousand lamas, or Buddhist priests, are supported at the expense of the Government. Nowhere does monstrous superstition exert a more baleful influence. True to the spirit of an heroic and historic past, the Moravians have planted their latest mission on the high lands of this interior and almost inaccessible country. For the first time, the sacred Scriptures have been translated into the language of the people. God grant that the handful of corn thus sown upon the top of the mountains may be fruitful as Lebanon, and that it may speedily flourish like grass of the earth!

China, "the Gibraltar of heathenism," also renders supreme homage to Buddha. Oriental religions, in their interlacings, are frequently intricate and difficult to trace. This is particularly the case in the Chinese empire. The earliest faith, as far as can be ascertained, in that part of Asia, was a plain and simple belief in the Supreme Being, creator of the heavens and the earth, and the beneficent and bountiful giver of all daily blessings. Monotheism was gradually obscured by materialistic worship—that of woods and rivers, hills and clouds. To this, as another distinguishing feature, was added the worship of ancestors. About five or six centuries before Christ, Lao-tze, an eminent teacher, propounded an elaborate system of philosophy; but, while failing to influence the masses through the medium of intellect, he encouraged polytheism and gross superstition. Thus he contributed greatly to the deepening of the spiritual gloom, and to the degeneracy of public worship. A still greater name in China is that of Confucius. For nearly twenty-five centuries the speculations and inculcations of this illustrious Sage have wielded a potent influence in that most populous land of the globe. Once a year, in official and representative character, accompanied by principal members of the court, the emperor of China renders national homage in the temple in Peking. "Confucius," he exclaims, "how great is Confucius!" The system of this venerated teacher, however, was a philosophy rather than a religion. His aim is thought to have been to rescue a primitive and comparatively pure religion from the corruptions of Taoism, to establish a rational worship, and to secure good government for the people. The central and controlling idea of Confucianism is that of subordination—of the wife to the husband, of the child to the parent, and of the subject to the sovereign. Obedience, if perfect, according to the original theory, would develop the five fundamental virtues: benevolence, uprightness, decorum, knowledge, and faithfulness. But the Sage of China failed to comprehend an inevitable law of fallen human nature: "When I would do good, evil is present with me." Hence the radical defect, and consequent failure, of the much-lauded system of morality. Theory was perfect. It is questionable if anything finer than the higher precepts of Confucius has ever emanated from any human source. But sublime inculcation was weak through the flesh.

Early in the Christian era Buddhism was promulgated in China, and may now be. regarded as the popular, if not the established, religion of the empire. It is difficult, however, to run any clear line of Chinese belief. Creeds are amalgamated, and worship is mixed. A Chinaman may hold three religions, if such they can be called, at one and the same time. Confucianism, Taoism and Buddhism are mingled in various proportions. The result is not a satisfactory one. There has been a long and continuous process of deterioration. Even Buddhism has degenerated. "It has never surmounted its environments, but, like organisms low in the scale of life, suffered those environments to modify its form, to tone down its abnormities, to eliminate elements too offensive to national taste and prejudices, and to incorporate other elements foreign to its constitution, yet essential to its survival."* Were

---

* Paper by Rev. F. T. Masters, Canton, 1882.

the Sakya-muni to return to earth, especially to those temples which bear his name in eastern and central Asia, he would scarcely pronounce a benediction on priest or people. Degrading idolatries obtain the sanction of the system, are sustained by the name and prestige of national worship, and almost everything in the form of an image or idol finds a place in Buddhist ceremonial and service.

Until forty years ago China was hermetically sealed. In that fact there may have been a providential design. The aggressive and conquering spirit of modern missions was preceded by days of spiritual feebleness. Overflowings of Chinese depravity might then have been sufficient to swamp all Christendom. It is always a great shock to the feelings of a Christian man or woman to be brought for the first time into contact with the institutions and immoralities of China, into which India has also poured so much of foulness and corruption. An interview with one or two missionaries, acquainted with coast and interior of the country, more than satisfies us in regard to the moral and spiritual condition of the teeming millions of people. China is one of the oldest countries in the world. It has long had the advantage of science and literature. Civilization is splendid. Education and other resources have been utilized and fully tested. But in spite of all this culture, it has, we are told, "become morally and socially worse and worse, until *the first chapter of Romans describes its condition,* as though written by a Chinaman." Testimony is all to the same purpose. We are assured that only personal contact can enable us to "realize how unutterably evil and miserable a thing heathenism is," and that "only One fully knows this." The Macedonian cry is intense and piercing, as when the heathen of Europe called to St. Paul, in the night-vision, "Come over and help us."

But signs of a good and gracious character are beginning to cheer the watchers and workers in that land. Missionaries are the men who know the country best, and they are hopeful in regard to the result. Traditional customs and beliefs will doubtless strive hard for the mastery, but the gospel must prevail. There is something better than Buddhism in store for China. Even the ancient Sage of the empire, through some snatch of Messianic prediction it may be, caught a glimpse of a brighter day: "In process of time a Holy One will be born, who will redeem the world. The nations will wait for him as the fading flowers desire the summer rain. He will be born of a virgin, and his name will be called the Prince of Peace. China will be visited by his glory." Then shall the sacred prophecy have its accomplishment: "And these shall come from far: and, lo, these from the north and the west; and these from the land of Sinim."

Buddhism is the popular religion of Japan, "the land of the rising sun." That country, with its thirty-five millions of people and a rapidly-advancing civilization, is destined probably to be the Great Britain of the Asiatic world. Shintoism, a kind of political and patriotic system, combining homage to the reigning sovereign with a form of ancestral worship, is the ancient Japanese religion, and until recently obtained State recognition. But there is little in it to meet or satisfy any of the instincts or aspirations of the human soul, and it now numbers comparatively few adherents. Buddhism is the religion of the mass. In 1869 it was represented by one hundred and sixty-eight thousand priests, and a vast number of temples and monasteries. But the Government has recently abolished the religious department of public service. This change, it is hoped, "will result in the final disendowment and overthrow of the old religions of the land."

A great change is passing over Japan. Her gates are being opened widely for the introduction of Western ideas. But religions, deeply founded in national sentiment, venerable by antiquity, buttressed by immense revenues, may not be expected to succumb readily to any rival. Adherents of an ancient system are not likely all at once to lose their faith in former guides. But that land of the sunrise needs a purer faith. Buddhism is responsible for very much of its darkness and superstition. It is not easy to lift the veil from the darker aspects even of civilized heathenism. When the first student from Japan was resident in the United States, a gentleman showed him an exquisitely formed and richly ornamented Japanese vase. It was regarded as a superb work of art, and a credit to the land of its production. He was asked to explain the mystic and elaborate characters and designs by which it was covered. But he had to remain silent,

for it displayed the deep shame of his country. That
beautifully wrought work of heathen Japan exhibited
"scenes and inscriptions breathing out impurity." No
wonder he longed for the gospel. It alone can lift
them "from the immoralities that pervade the land,
and leave a stain on all they touch." But a new sun
has risen; and as foul things shrink from the light,
the shadows of a long, deep night shall flee away.

The ports of Japan were opened to trade in 1854,
and her doors to missionaries in 1869. The political
changes which preceded and produced this remarkable
revolution could not be regarded as the result of human
foresight and wisdom. The Japanese have been, unconsciously on their part, led to a consummation of
which, at the outset, they never dreamed. It has been
as in the vision of the Hebrew prophet. The mystic
chariot of providential movement, as seen at Chebar,
was wide in its sweep. There was an apparently
complicated motion, as of "a wheel in the middle of a
wheel." But the wheels of revolution were guided by
infallible wisdom; and there was rapid and continuous
progress, for "they turned not when they went."

While doors were being strangely opened in Japan,
there was a simultaneous preparation of agency. At
a time when a heavy penalty was attached to leaving
the country, in 1865, young Joseph Neesima ran away
to Shanghai, and there obtained a passage to Boston.
He had a passionate desire to learn to read, and his
first lessons were received from the sailors. Through
the earlier part of John's Gospel he patiently pursued

his way. The sixteenth verse of the third chapter arrested his attention. It was a wonderful announcement: "For God so loved the world, that he gave his only begotten Son, that whosoever believeth in him should not perish, but have everlasting life." The sense and significance of that glorious passage began to dawn slowly on his mind, and he prayed for light and truth. Through the interest of the captain, on their arrival at Boston, he was introduced to the generous owner of the vessel, and sent in course to Phillip's Academy and Amherst College. He graduated, had flattering offers to remain in the United States, but nobly persisted in his purpose to return and preach the gospel to his countrymen. This youthful student went home to Japan, "possessed of the zeal of an apostle," and is now at the head of an influential institution in Tokio, for the purpose of training young men for the work of the Christian ministry.

Buddhism is still a mighty force in Japan. Immense sums are just now being expended on its structures. But the proudest and palmiest days are past. A missionary visited Kioto, the sacred capital, in 1873, and recorded his impressions of the waning power of the national religion. It had not then received impulse and stimulus from the rivalry of an active and aggressive evangelistic movement. Decadence was everywhere manifest. He wandered all one afternoon among the ancient and beautiful Buddhist temples on the east of Kioto. Paths and walks leading up to and around the sacred places were grass-grown and deserted. Even the priests had forsaken the shrine. Wandering through the halls and corridors, as among solitary ruins, he "could not refrain from thinking and wishing and praying for men ready to go up and possess the land."

One of the most remarkable things about the intellectual uprising in Japan, is the earnest attempt to grapple with the perplexing problems of modern thought. Japanese scholars read ponderous works of philosophy and science. We hear that their orders, including productions of Herman Lotze, Kant, Darwin, Huxley, Herbert Spencer, and Stuart Mill, are the surprise of booksellers. "Not a wave," it is said, "of religious error or advance, not a schism, not a doubt, not a protest, is started on the current of American or English thought, but breaks on that shore." The rationalism of cultured classes presents a formidable obstacle to the diffusion of evangelical truth. Churches at home have need to pray earnestly for their missionaries in Japan.

But the axe is laid to the root of the tree of Buddhism, and it shall be hewn down and cast into the fire. Before coffee can be grown in Ceylon a dense forest growth must be stripped and cleared from the hills. The workmen commence at the foot of the slope. Trees are usually entangled in a profusion of climbing plants, and this luxuriance of tropical foliage must be first removed. Then the lowest tree is nearly, but not quite, cut through. Numerous fellers repeat the process, and ere long the crowning ridge is reached. The topmost tree is then cut through at its root, and, as it falls, bears down the one beneath. Others fall in their turn, and crash follows crash until all the trees are prostrate. Analogous processes are going on in the realm of Oriental idolatry. Through Ceylon and China, Burmah and Japan, a few stately trees have fallen, and the reverberations of the woodman's axe begin to sound across the Asiatic continent. But more labourers are called for, and native fellers need to be raised up. Jungles of heathen superstition and hoary idolatries shall echo to the ringing strokes of many sharp and gleaming axes. Heathenism shall be destroyed, and a purer growth promoted. "Instead of the thorn shall come up the fir tree, and instead of the brier shall come up the myrtle tree."

"At times, too, dark suspicions will cross the mind that such inferior races as those of Africa are not suited for so pure and elevated a religion as that of Christ, and that the best service they could render to the Christianization of the world would be to die out and become extinct. We must not, however, give heed to thoughts like these. We must believe, rather, that God has made of one blood all the nations of men that dwell upon the earth."— *Missionary Record.*

IV.

UNCIVILIZED HEATHENISM: AFRICA AND ISLES OF THE SEA.

IN lands of Brahmanical and Buddhistic superstition, and of idolatrous religions, we have been in contact with the structures of an ancient and splendid civilization. But there is also an uncivilized heathenism. Through its dark and deceptive shadows, multitudes of sinning and suffering people are groping their way to an endless future. The Macedonian cry of benighted millions appeals to and arouses the conscience and compassion of a long-slumbering and apathetic Church. Tribes at the lowest level of civilization are members of the one human family, and belong to a common brotherhood. "God hath made of one blood all nations of men, for to dwell on all the face of the earth; and hath determined the times before appointed, and the bounds of their habitation."

Thought turns to Africa: "an immense and homogeneous continent, groaning under the curse of the slave-trade, the darkness of superstition, already half of it under the yoke of Islam; before whose estuaries long sand-banks stretch beneath the heavy surf; whose interior is encircled by the broad, rainless belt of the Sahara; while the entrances are at all points barred by the deadly fevers of a tropical climate."*

A quarter of a century ago, the interior of Africa was an almost unexplored region, a blank space on the map of that continent. It was generally believed to consist largely of burning desert sands, and of immense and pathless wastes, unfit for human habitation. Even members of the African Association spoke of it as "unlike other continents" of the earth; no large inland lakes, or broad rolling rivers flowing from the centre to the extremities. But, in the interests of Christianity, science, and commerce, the enterprise of numerous explorers has done much to dispel the mystery of the Dark Continent. Until recently unknown regions have been mapped out with scientific precision. The source of the Nile, for three thousand years the problem of African geography, through intrepidity of explorers, has been traced to equatorial lakes and mountains. A broad belt of low land, fraught with miasma and fever, skirts the coast; and as missions continued for a long period to be confined mainly to the unhealthy margin, they were prosecuted at a fearful sacrifice of life. But the configuration and climate of intertropical Africa are not what had been once supposed. Within the lines of the fever-belt, flanked on the east and west by longitudinal ridges, the country forms a vast table-land, depressed to the lake region at the centre. The explorer finds himself richly rewarded as he

---

* Christlieb's *Foreign Missions*, p. 101.

reaches that upland plateau. There are glimpses of undulating and magnificent stretches of country, covered with tall grass, dotted by clumps of superb foliage, threaded by silver streams, bathed in floods of pure and brilliant sunlight, and bounded by distant and dark mountain masses. Almost boundless capabilities of material wealth awaits an immediate development, and the enterprises of Christianity should at least keep pace with the advance and achievements of commerce and science.

The mission field of Africa may be regarded as forming several distinct and very different sections.

A narrow northern strip, bordering on the Mediterranean, extending from Morocco to Egypt, was at one time the seat of empire, the source of flourishing commerce, and the site of influential Christian churches. But the Vandal conquerors of Rome crossed the Straits of Gibraltar, and laid the country waste from west to east. From the period of barbarian invasion, that border land never recovered the strength or splendor of an earlier civilization. Under the standard of the Saracen, by which the Barbary States were next swept and completely subjugated, the religion of the Koran was remorselessly promulgated. Mohammedanism is still the dominant creed. The mixed races of people, a fusion of Arabian and Libyan blood, with more than a trace of the ancient Phenician, are possessed of splendid natural capabilities; and, in the day of Africa's redemption, they are sure to take a foremost place.

Western Africa extends from Morocco and Senegambia to the south as far as the Bight of Benin. Back from the belt of western coast lies the great slave region of Soudan, where eighty million of people have sunk to the very lowest level of degradation and misery. Of the actual and pitiable condition of the populations distant from the sea, we have only faint and occasional glimpses. Thick mists of obscurity, especially in the direction of the river Niger, hang heavily and gloomily over the interior country. But even if the veil were lifted, density dispelled, and the barbarities of life fully understood, it is scarcely probable that there would be anything to relieve the dark and dismal picture.

Facts of Slave Coast atrocities, the story of which has been repeatedly told, have caused the civilized world to shudder; and, in the name of a common humanity, such vile observances have been denounced and execrated. Dahomian annual " customs " are signalized by processions, revelling and intoxication, the horrid sound of the fatal drum, an exhibition of skulls, and a parade of barbaric trophies. A national ceremonial, in which the immolation of eighty of the sanguinary monarch's subjects contributed to the *eclat* of the occasion, was witnessed and described by Captain Burton. Grand customs are performed on the death of the king; and, at such a time, hundreds of men and women fall victims to " revenge, ostentation and pretended piety." The number of persons slaughtered in cold blood, when these abominable rites were celebrated in 1860, was estimated at *more than two thousand*. Assuredly the dark places of the earth are full of the habitations of cruelty.

A vivid remembrance of early life is connected with the perusal of Freeman's famous missionary journal. It contained a glowing narrative of his first visit to Ashanti, and of the scenes which he witnessed in the blood-stained streets of Kumasi. An immense procession paraded the prominent places of the capital. In that motley mass and array, the royal executioners found a conspicuous position. Instead of streaming banners and proud insignia and the kind of pomp and pageantry to which we are accustomed in the civil and military processions of Christian and civilized countries, instruments of torture and decapitation were ostentatiously displayed. There was the diabolical death-drum, literally covered with dried clots of blood, and decorated with human skulls. It was always beaten when the cold and cruel steel had done its work, and the heads of unfortunate victims had been severed from their bodies. No less than forty lives were sacrificed during a space of two days. The ground was saturated with blood, and "putrefying bodies tainted the air." That daring and heroic visit had been undertaken for the purpose of effecting an entrance for the gospel. No wonder that the solitary missionary, as he gazed upon the slaughtered victims of relentless and capricious ferocity, was filled with sorrow and indignation, and longed for the means of amelioration. The very stones of the blood-drenched streets cried out for help. Could there be any response to that Macedonian wail? From Kumasi, the dark and deluded capital of Ashanti, the thought of the missionary turned to the metropolis of Christian England. In contrast to immediate and sanguinary surroundings, another and far different scene burst upon his vision. Was it all a fancy, or did it breathe the promise of an assuring hope? Exeter Hall is in a flame. Missions are eloquently advocated. Voices are raised in behalf of dark Africa. Emotion finds expression in "a hymn for the heathen," and the prayer of the great congregation ascends to God in heaven:

> "The servile progeny of Ham
> Seize as the purchase of thy blood."

No, that is not all an illusion! The missionary has faith to believe that the enthusiasm of such a meeting is genuine, the altar-fire pure, and that Christian people are in earnest. But the holy impulse largely passes away with the occasion. There has been too much of timidity and delay in spiritual enterprise. "O righteous Father," the Saviour was impelled to exclaim, "the world hath not known thee." . "O compassionate Redeemer," might have been the sorrowful strain of the Kumasi missionary, "thy Church is straitened in her sympathies, indifferent to her great commission, forgetful of thy claims and crown-rights, and too long heedless of the Macedonian cry from this perishing world."

The west coast of Africa, and especially Sierra Leone, has been designated "the missionary's grave." Thirty laborers of the Church Missionary Society, during the first twelve years, fell bravely at their post, and were laid to rest in the burial-ground of the mission church. A wasted remnant of the Basle Society's missionaries, in one fatal year, had to stand by the fresh graves of ten of their stricken brethren. Forty Wesleyan pioneers fell in rapid succession in the same field:

> "For dangers uncounted are clustering there,
>   The pestilence stalks uncontrolled,
>   Strange poisons are borne on the soft languid air,
>   And lurk in each leaf's fragrant fold."

But the missionary succession has been nobly maintained. As repeated gaps have been made in the ranks, new men have filled up the vacant spaces, and the consecrated banner has been seized from hands that had stiffened in death. The gifted and spiritual Melville B. Coxe, who went out in 1833, was not alone in his faith and fortitude. He spoke of going to "a land of sickness," and stipulated that if he should die a friend of his youth should come and write his epitaph. But "what shall I write?" was the inquiry of the Christian brother. The impassioned missionary was prompt in reply: "Write, though a thousand fall, let Africa live!" In a few months this heroic and heavenly-minded messenger of the cross finished his brief course, and his body found a resting-place in the land of swamp and fever. Such losses have been keenly felt. But the dust of the mission graveyards along the line of that baleful coast is precious and full of promise. For long centuries the sepulchre of patriarchs in Canaan was the only pledge to the covenant people, and the assurance that they should go up and possess the promised land. Burial-places in which the dust of missionaries and of members of their families has been rendered to the mould is the consecration of many a heathen land.

The subject of mission effort and enterprise, on the western coast of Africa, has an aspect of encouragement and hope. Light has been shot into this "darkest dungeon of the planet." From the Gambia to the Gaboon, a distance of two thousand miles, an infamous traffic in human flesh and blood has been brought to an end. Slave-pens have been transformed into marts of legitimate traffic. One of the earliest missionary erections, a spacious old sanctuary, that has long echoed the strains of praise to God, was framed and sheathed out of the beams and planks of a condemned slaver. Thousands of people along an extended line of coast have heard the glad tidings of salvation, and have been the subjects of a blessed spiritual emancipation. There seemed to be a dark day for Africa in 1822, and signs ominous of a deeper bondage, as a slave-ship sped out full sail through the lagoon of Lagos; a sinister-looking hulk, packed with human beings, destined for the Brazil market. But a cruiser crossed her path, and the boom of a British gun said to the slaver, "Yield up thy prey." Among the slaves of that crowded cargo was an entire family, father and mother, boys and girls, ruffianly torn from their homes. A bright boy from that group was sent to a school in Sierra Leone. He was early converted to God, became an explorer, a successful evangelist, and ultimately was entrusted with episcopal responsibilities. Noble in physique, eloquent in speech, and fervent in spirit, the venerable Crowther is one of the greatest and most apostolic of missionary bishops; and his flourishing diocese, containing the home of his childhood, extends far as the Niger and the Benone.

The work along the line of the Gold and Slave Coasts, prosecuted at a great cost of men and means, has not been in vain in the Lord. Once it was affirmed that the whole region was merely a vast moral savannah, a dense steaming swamp, and that from such rank and reeking plains of atrocity, vileness, and superstition, no harvest of golden sheaves could ever be gathered. But, in looking upon such a scene of widespread and appalling misery and helpless woe, Christian people have been led to realize the need of a deeper dependence upon Divine aid, and of a supreme consecration to the service of God. Missionary faith has never failed or faltered. Sometimes the shadows hide the heaviest wheat of all. The grain is already ripe, and the reaper must thrust in his sickle and reap, or it will rot to the ground. "Say not ye, there are yet four months, and then cometh the harvest? Behold I say unto you, Lift up your eyes, and look on the fields; for they are white already to harvest.

And he that reapeth receiveth wages, and gathereth fruit unto life eternal: that both he that soweth and he that reapeth may rejoice together."

The southern section of the African continent comprises Bushmen, Kaffirs, Zulus, Matalabe, Namaquas, and other tribes to the north of the Orange River. South Africa was early selected as a field of missionary enterprise. Beginning from the Cape colony, the work of evangelization was rapidly pushed to the interior of the country. Through the agency and influence, the patience and statesmanlike sagacity, of such men as Robert Moffat, William Shaw, and pioneers of the Moravian and other societies, a bright and imperishable record has been secured. When these men, and others of like consecrated spirit and purpose, commenced their missionary course, there was a serious doubt even in the minds of some Christian people as to the capacity of African tribes for the reception of the gospel, or for elevation in the scale of civilization. It was proposed by Mr. Moffat to a Dutch settler, in whose house he had obtained permission to preach, that some of the servants should be brought in to the service. "What," roared the burly Boer, who had a hundred of the despised outcasts of all the tribes at his command, "preach to the Hottentots! You may as well go to the mountains and preach to the baboons; or, if you like, I'll fetch my dogs, and you may preach to them." The missionary had intended to announce the "great salvation" from the standpoint of an inspired and solemn question. But, prompt to seize the incident of the occasion, the words of the Syrophenician suppliant were selected for a theme: "Truth, Lord; yet the dogs eat of the crumbs which fall from their master's table." The teaching of Christ was elucidated, and the subject was searchingly applied. "No more of that," pleaded the softened Boer, "I will bring in all the Hottentots in the place."

Benighted bushmen have since then been brought to hear of Jesus and his love, and have been made the recipients of a common salvation. Some of the most treasured trophies of the South African Missions have been won from the families of this scattered and politically insignificant race. Latent genius for song has found a remarkable development. At the dedication of a bushland place of worship, erected under missionary auspices, a choir of bush negroes, assisted by converted slaves from the colony, signalized the occasion by strains of music that would have enriched cathedral worship. They sang with fervor, fine sense of appreciation and good effect, a selection from Haydn's magnificent oratorio of the "Creation," "the Heavens are Telling." Thus a grand chorus which moves cultured and select audiences at home, and thrills to an indescribable emotion, broke the silence of an African wilderness, and filled with rapture the souls of converted Hottentot worshippers. Who could have supposed, even when touched and transformed by the power of Divine grace, that these servile wanderers had the ability to achieve success in a delicate and difficult sphere? Shall not these ransomed sons and daughters of the bushland, taught to praise the Saviour's name on earth, one day form part of a heavenly choir, and there sing unto him that hath loved them and washed them from their sins in his own blood?

Ten long and trying years, the apostolic Moffat spent among the barbarous and benighted Namaquas and his missionary faith and purpose were sorely tested. But ultimately he was cheered by a success that revealed the glorious possibilities of mission work. "At length they listened, at last began to tremble, and finally wept; repenting of sin, they forsook it; and hearing of the gospel, they believed it."

Bushmen and Namaquas, in their native degradation, hold a low place in the average qualities of manhood. But South Africa has races possessed of superb capabilities of which she may well be proud. Kaffirs and Zulus have encountered the best and bravest of British troops, and have proved themselves to be no contemptible foes. Bechuanas maintain their independence, and give evidence of progressive ability. But over all this region, at the commencement of missionary enterprise, there rested the deep and settled gloom of an uncivilized heathenism. The people walked in darkness and dwelt in the land of the shadow of death. Fierce and warlike races delighted in blood and rapine. No traveller with safety could pass through the borders of any of these tribes, for the people were habitually cruel and treacherous.

An ordinary occurrence may indicate the general condition of the country on the arrival of the earliest European missionaries. The kraal or cattle-fold of a South African village is surrounded by grass or reed-thatched huts, resembling the corn-stacks of a farm yard. In that enclosure the chief assembles his people: warriors in the centre, and the women and children on the outer circle. By a rude but stirring eloquence he moves the barbarian horde, fires the martial spirit of the men, and prepares them for any plundering excursion. The eye of the speaker dilates, and his voice becomes tremulous with passion and excitement. Distant hills visible upon the horizon are the home of a peaceful and prosperous people, with multitudes of flocks, and herds of sheep and oxen, but "their hearts are white as milk." In their sense of security they may be easily vanquished. Exultant response greets the fierce appeal. An attack is at once agreed upon, and, armed for murderous deed, troops march the same night. Beneath the streaming starlight, they move stealthily across the intervening plain, and reach the hills at early dawn. A savage shout startles the encampment. There is slender resistance, for the people have been taken by surprise. Men, women, and children are slaughtered without mercy. Houses are fired, and the village swept by a general conflagration. Cattle are driven off, and the victors bearing their spoil are welcomed back with shout and triumph. The heart sickens at the thought of such atrocities, but this was the normal condition of an immense extent of territory. Whether the fittest always survived in the treacheries of warfare may be open to question. Whole tribes were exterminated. Human life was lightly regarded, and it is only a matter of surprise that such sanguinary struggles had not long ago depopulated the whole land.

South African tribes in their savage state seem to have been literally without any knowledge of God. It is said that when pioneer missionaries first began to speak concerning the existence of a Supreme Being, of the fall and the entrance of sin into the world, of the incarnation and sacrificial work of the Redeemer, of the resurrection and the hope of immortality, their statements were regarded as fabulous and as little to be believed as were native exaggerations concerning lions and wild beasts of the jungle. But the most barbarous of savages have a conscience that may be reached by the light of truth. To a fierce chief Mr. Moffat spoke of resurrection and future judgment. The idea was new and tremendous even to a heathen mind. "What," he exclaimed, "are these words about? Will my father arise? Will all the dead slain in battle arise? Hark, ye wise men, whoever is wise among you, the wisest of past generations, did ever your ears hear such strange news?" But as the light of revelation dawned upon his savage mind, and conscience spoke of deeds of rapine and murder, appalled by the thought of meeting the victims of many heartless cruelties, the barbarian sought to silence the missionaries. "The words of the resurrection," he said, "are too great to be heard. I do not want to hear about the dead arising. The dead cannot arise; they must not arise."

For South Africa the day dawns! Darkness of heathenism is being gradually dispersed by the advancing light of Christianity. Manifold are the evidences of amelioration. Regions through which once white men dare not attempt to travel are now intersected by safe thoroughfares. Churches and cultivated lands furnish evidence of religion and of prosperous industry. Unwritten sounds have been gathered up and formed into a grammatical language. The Bible has been given to Kaffir and Bechuana, and thousands of natives are able to read the Old and New Testaments. At Kurumen the sable compositors in the printing office are the very men who a few years before would have been grasping the blood-stained spear, and revelling in deeds of slaughter. In the early days of mission effort a few enterprizing traders penetrated to the heart of an uncivilized territory. But the very idea of traffic was turned to scorn, and not a single purchaser could be found. Now, European manufactures to the value of three or four hundred thousand pounds sterling annually pass through the mission stations into the interior, imported and exchanged by the people who a few years ago had no conception of the utility of commerce.*

To the men and women who led the van of evan-

---

* See Rev. Dr. Moffat's address at Mildmay Conference, 1878.

gelization, exhibited the power and purity of the religion of Jesus, set to the savages around them an example of the sweetness and attractiveness of a Christian home, inculcated and exemplified the spirit and precepts of peace and goodwill, translated the sacred Scriptures and laid the foundation of a native literature, secured the erection of commodious places of worship and the establishment of efficient schools, trained a native agency to such an extent that were every foreign missionary to retire from the field the work would still go on—to the founders of this great and glorious movement we accord the recognition that is due to saints and heroes. Their names shall be had in everlasting remembrance.

The explorer of Eastern and Equatorial Africa enters a new and densely-populated region. A spacious and magnificent territory, abounding in material resources, can scarcely be surpassed in any other part of the world. Apparently it is a rich reserve for the African race, and seems designed by Providence for some future and marvellous development. But the deep shadows of heathen superstition rest upon this land, and upon its interesting races the blight and desolation and unmitigated curse of slavery have heavily fallen. Through means of an inhuman traffic in flesh and blood, with all its accompanying evils, scenes of almost Eden loveliness have been changed to pandemonium. This sum of all villanies is at its worst in the interior of Africa. Hunting parties, selected from the more warlike tribes, are furnished with firearms by Arabian slave dealers. As the ordinary weapons of the natives are bows and arrows, a murderous musketry fire produces an immediate panic. There is no alternative in the customary raid but to fly and be shot down, or to stand and submit to a bondage worse than death. Many scenes of horror were witnessed by Dr. Livingstone. They were pathetically said to "harden all within and petrify the feelings;" and, as he beheld the "tears of such as were oppressed and had no comforter," he could find no relief except in the remembrance that "He that is higher than the highest regardeth." An incident lifts the veil from fearful outrages upon common rights of humanity. One of the finest of the interior tribes has a home on the banks of the beautiful Lualaba river. The market-place is a wonted resort for amusement and social intercourse. One day an armed half-caste and sinister-looking Arab, and a band of ruffian followers, came suddenly into the midst of this peaceable and pleasant scene. Suspicion was at once excited, and the worst fears were speedily realized. Beneath the whole heavens a more villanous deed was not to be witnessed than that which was suddenly enacted on that sultry summer morning. Deadly fire was opened upon the helpless crowd, and volley succeeded volley with terrible effect. Gaps were rapidly made in the mass of two thousand human beings, and slaughter was indiscriminate. Through the murderous bullet of the assailant, or by plunging into the deep river, hundreds lost their lives. "Shot after shot continued to be fired on the helpless and perishing. Some of the long line of heads disappeared quietly" beneath the water; "whilst other poor creatures threw up their arms, as if appealing to the great Father above, and sank." Villages were set on fire. "As I write I hear the loud wails on the left bank over those who are slain, ignorant of their many friends now in the Lualaba. O, let thy kingdom come!"*

The extent to which this infernal business is carried on, and the enormity of the evil, may be inferred from the fact that no less than fifteen thousand agents are employed by one flourishing Egyptian city, Khartoum. They are engaged solely for the purpose of ensnaring and enslaving human beings. Marching through the night, in some part of the Nile basin, they steal upon an unsuspecting village, and fire the grass huts. As the sleeping occupants seek to escape from their flaming habitations, the men are shot down, and the women and children are secured as slaves. The necks of mothers and maidens are thrust into a forked wooden pole and securely lashed, while the children are attached by ropes, and thus a living chain is formed. By secret paths the pitiable procession marches to the coast. There, like bales of merchandise, the almost heart-broken captives are crowded together into the hot and stifling air of the pestilential slave-dhow. There is a dreary uniformity in the main facts of African slavery. "The tale was almost invariably one

---
* Dr. Livingstone's *Last Journals*, July 14th, 1871.

of surprise, kidnapping, and generally of murder—always of indescribable suffering on the way down to the coast and on the dhow voyage."* Then, it has been affirmed that for each marketable slave that reaches the sea-board, at least ten lives are lost in the interior of the country. It is estimated that, through the territory of the Zambesi and Shire rivers, the Lake Nyassa, the Rovuma, and other hunting grounds, during a long and uninterrupted period, this vile traffic involved annually the death of half a million of human beings. Details such as these are saddening and sickening to thought and feeling. But they belong to the sum of Africa's wrongs, and give meaning to the Macedonian cry, "Come over and help us." These facts enable us in some measure to realize the nature of missionary obligation: "to bind up the broken-hearted, to proclaim liberty to the captive, and the opening of the prison to them that are bound."

Eastern and Central African missions are comparatively in their infancy. But the beneficent effects of evangelical agency and influence are already apparent. The slave market at Zanzibar, which received annually, and passed over to Arab traffickers, from twenty to twenty-five thousand persons, has been broken up,

---

* Sir Bartle Frere. For the main facts connected with the "East African Slave-Trade," the deeds of Arab traffickers in human flesh and blood, the markets in which slaves are sold, and countries, chiefly Mohammedan, through which the captured Africans are dispersed, see "Report on Sir Bartle Frere's Mission to Zanzibar," presented to both Houses of Parliament, 1873.

and selected as the site of the Universities' mission premises. Cheering tidings reach us that the Livingstonia enterprise has succeeded in stopping the slave-trade around the seven hundred miles of the Lake Nyassa coast; from which, in former times, accompanied by all the atrocities of the system, nineteen thousand slaves were annually carried off. "All I can add in my loneliness," said Dr. Livingstone, as he sorrowed for the wrongs of the captive, " may heaven's rich blessing come down upon every one, American, English, or Turk, who will help to heal *the open sore of the world!*" * These touching words of the great missionary explorer have been appropriately inscribed on his tomb in Westminster Abbey; and through these, as the best friend of Africa, " he being dead yet speaketh."

The people of Central Africa give promise of capability for improvement. Dr. Livingstone's judgment was rarely at fault, for sympathy with humanity in all its forms only quickened his perception, and his estimate of the interior tribes was almost always favorable. Nsama's people, resident in the lovely country to the west of Lake Tanganyika, are enthusiastically described. Many of them are said to be handsome in form and feature, and to exhibit as perfect a phrenological development as could be seen in an European assembly. An impression that the true type of negro was to be found in the ancient

---

* Blaikie's *Life of Dr. Livingstone*, p. 454.

Egyptian, rather than in the coarse ugliness of the West Coast, received abundant confirmation. " The African races are of a type different from what Europeans are accustomed to associate with high and polished civilization, and undoubtedly some of their customs are barbarian; but the African races are open to be toned down, modified, and improved upon as were the primitive customs of Europe." *

Central Africa is all a surprise. Instead of a dreary waste of burning and unsheltered sand, as had been supposed, it has broad lakes and rolling rivers, healthy uplands, and a rich tropical foliage. And it is quite as marvellous a thing, where the traveller had expected to come into contact with inferior types of the human family, to meet the swarthy but comely children of the sun, dwellers by the great inland seas. To the African races a noble continent has been assigned, and we cannot but believe that a great future is in reserve for christianized Africa.

In the earlier period of the world's history, physical force prevailed. Men of sinew and muscle commanded distinction. Then came the age of intellectual achievement. Mental qualities and attributes still exercise a dominating influence. But are there no intimations of a purely moral and spiritual superiority? Are we not possibly nearing a time when culture of the soul, graces of character, and the beauty of holiness shall win the most genuine admiration? Then shall Africa

---

* *Contemporary Review*, December, 1882.

have her turn! In many attractive qualities, susceptibility of moral nature, exuberance of feeling, fervor of passion, intensity of affection, glow of enthusiasm, love of music, ecstasy of song, instincts of religion, and rapture of devotion, the finer type of the negro race, as found in the populous lake region, can scarcely be surpassed. Surely the day of redemption draws nigh! Relieved from slavery, purified through faith, ennobled by Christian culture, a long-despised people may come to furnish some of the best and most beautiful specimens of a sanctified humanity. Swarthy tribes shall rise in the scale of an exalted civilization. Right and rank, in council and congress, will be recognized and awarded. Europa and other leading members of the great human family can then welcome the long exiled one, and say, "It was meet that we should be glad: for this our sister was dead, and is alive again: and was lost, and is found."

Everywhere the light is breaking! A period of dreary monotony is passing away, never to return. Unexpected facilities are afforded to travel and traffic. The Nile and the Niger, the Congo and the Coanza, the Zambesi and the Shire, and other great rivers, form magnificent natural highways to the very heart of the continent. Nor is it easy for us to grasp the significance of such a fact. The mighty Congo alone, with its tributaries, drains an enormous and densely populated region of eighty thousand square miles. On central lakes, the Nyassa, the Tanganyika, and the Victoria Nyanza, steam and other forces of civilization begin to be utilized in the interests of religion and commerce. It is worthy of remembrance and record that missionaries have been amongst the foremost and most heroic of African pioneers. They have mostly formed the vanguard of this great movement of the century; and when the history of human progress shall have been written, many a page shall glow with the splendor of their names. But such achievements are all too great for the chronicles of earth, and doubtless they are inscribed before the eternal throne.

The area of uncivilized heathenism is not bounded exclusively by the limits of the Dark Continent. Deep shadows still rest upon adjacent territory, and lie thick beneath the bending Southern Cross. From Africa we turn to the Isles of the Sea. Off from the African coast, across the Mozambique Channel, lies the magnificent island of Madagascar. Until a few years ago, it was the scene of darkest heathenism. "So you will make the Malagasy Christians," said the Governor of a French island to the pioneer missionaries. "Impossible! They are brutes, and have no more sense than irrational cattle." But the martyr Church of Madagascar has won and now worthily wears the crown of modern spiritual heroism. In 1836, the last of a brave missionary cohort, Johns and Baker, by the merciless edict of the heathen Queen Ranavalona, were driven from the capital and the island. But amongst the native converts were some that exhibited an extraordinary courage and steadfastness of purpose and profession. Though forsaken, they still met for religious worship. Foremost of this noble band was Rafaravavy, a lady distinguished for intelligence, rare beauty, and great purity of character. She and her companions sometimes walked a distance of twenty miles into the hill country; and there, amidst the sounding aisles of the dim woods, or on the calm mountain summit, they sang hymns of praise to God. But furious persecutors were on their track. The gifted and gentle leader of the Christian company of confessors was put in irons, bearing the significant name of "causing many tears." Records of the little Malagasy Church began to be written in blood. Multitudes of people were summoned by the roar of cannon to gaze upon scenes of suffering and endurance, which the annals of martyrdom had nothing to surpass. Men and women, because of the steadfastness of their Christian faith, bound in cords, wrapped in soiled matting, choked with rags to prevent their testimony, were committed to the flames, or hurled from the edge of the sharp Ampamarinana rocks. During those days of fiery persecution, many converts obtained the crown of martyrdom, and went up to join the noble army of martyrs before the throne of God. "*More Christians were put to death than there were Christians on the island when the persecutions commenced and the missionaries were banished!*"

But thirteen years ago, heathenism was suddenly hurled from its barbarous and bloody throne. Another and a nobler Queen, Ranavalona, burnt the national idols, and publicly expressed her preference for the Christian religion. Her coronation mottoes were mainly selected from the Malagasy version of the Holy Scriptures: " Glory to God," " Peace on earth," " Goodwill to men," " God with us." Idolatry was suddenly abandoned. Idols were brought by thousands from their houses into the street or square, and there consumed to ashes. Slavery has since been abolished by royal proclamation. National legislation is permeated by the spirit of Divine precept. Madagascar now stands out to the view of the Church and the world as a glorious monument of what the gospel of Jesus Christ can speedily accomplish for the purity, elevation, and salvation of an uncivilized heathen people.

There are other dark places in the heathen world. The demon-worship of the Battas, amongst the mountain ranges of Sumatra; the cannibalism of the dark and roaming Dyaks, which pollutes the fragrant groves of beautiful Borneo; the degrading superstitions of the natives of New Guinea, in the Southern Pacific; and other abominations of uncivilized heathenism abundantly illustrate the annals of human depravity. But, on the face of the earth, there are not to be found tribes or races of people more utterly vile and inhumanized than many of those that have already been sought out and evangelized.

Once New Zealand was regarded as one of the least promising of missionary fields. Samuel Marsden and Samuel Leigh, in 1813 and 1819, went there as the pioneers of Church of England and Wesleyan missions. They had to witness unnameable atrocities and abominations. The people were savage cannibals. A single incident may suffice for illustration. Two rival chiefs, Hongi and Hinaki, met in deadly feud, and Hinaki was slain. The conqueror, Hongi, sprang forward instantly and scooped out and swallowed the dying warrior's eye; and then, plunging his knife into the throat of his victim, he filled his hand with the copiously-flowing blood, and drank it with exulting satisfaction. What a contrast do we find in the case of an old New Zealand chief, converted in middle life! He lived consistently; and, when his last end drew near, gathered his friends around him, and sang an ancient song of his country. But all knew that the words had a new meaning, and that they were transfigured into the light of the gospel. A maiden in search of her lover went out in her frail canoe. She went down the dark river, and on to fast and foaming rapids. Steep rocks closed in on either side, and through the black pass the waters flowed into a wide sea. But still the maiden was not afraid, for she looked forward all the more to a meeting with him she loved so well. Thus the dying chief told how the currents of life were mingling with the ocean of eternity. But he feared no evil. To die was gain. The bark of his immortal spirit would soon reach the shining shore, and he would be with the blessed Saviour forever.

When John Hunt and his heroic wife landed on the shores of Fiji, the captain of the vessel was compelled in self-defence to put loaded muskets into the hands of his men. Nature was robed in almost peerless beauty. The sky was serene, and a sea of crystal clearness laved the coral strand. Islands were fringed with an exquisite tropical foliage. If there was an elysium on earth, it must surely be here! But man was vile beyond description. The tall and ferocious savages, with painted bodies and bushy heads, a spear in one hand and a club in the other, that rushed down to the shore, were probably fresh from a cannibal feast, and ready for any shuddering deed of inhumanity. At that time whole villages were depopulated, to provide human flesh for the constantly recurring repast. The language of that group contains no word for corpse, but one that signifies "a body to be eaten." Fiji "islanders had a bad reputation over all other heathen people." Their abominations were unnameable. The Rev. Robert Young, who went as a missionary deputation to "the Southern World" in 1853, in reminiscences of his visit, depicts many a dark scene. After a reference to Lakemba and Viwa, he tells how he proceeded to Mbau, the capital of the country, and "doubtless the greatest hell upon earth." Six ovens were shown to him in which eighteen human beings had been recently cooked, in order to provide a feast for some distinguished stranger. Remains of the horrid repast were still to be seen. A large stone at the door of one of the heathen temples, against which the heads of many victims had been dashed, still bore the marks of blood. No wonder that the pen faltered, and that the writer was compelled to pause in his narrative. "There are scenes of wickedness, forms of cannibalism and depravity in that country which cannot be told." Dire were the doings of heathen Fiji. But what an amazing change has been wrought! That group of islands has been christianized, ceded to Great Britain, and constitutes the advanced post of her commerce in the Southern Pacific. A distinguished naval officer, during a visit to those islands, noted striking way-marks of progress. At a religious service, conducted with reverence and spiritual feeling, it was known that every man present had been a cannibal up to fifteen years of that time. A venerable-looking chief, once the most sanguinary and ferocious in that terrible land, Bible in hand and spectacles on forehead, followed the subject with eager and devout interest. There was a fatal oven, not twenty yards away, in which human bodies had been baked for the savage feast. A tree, covered with notches, to mark the number of victims, still perpetuated a record of dark and evil deeds. And yet, according to the testimony of the late Governor, Sir Arthur Gordon, "the people of Fiji are now a Christian people."

A missionary of the London Society, in contrast with a later scene, graphically describes a first night spent in New Guinea. On this earlier occasion there were fires gleaming through the groves of cocoa-nut trees. The evening was soft, but the sultry air thrilled with the cries of helpless women. Heathenism, in its foulest and most repulsive forms of cannibalism and murderous rage, was all around, and there was none to help or restrain. Seven years later, in the course of which the softening and transforming power of the gospel had been experienced, he noted the change. There was the gleam of fires in the same cocoa grove. But instead of shrieks there were sweet songs of praise to the Redeemer. Converted natives love their hymn books. They were now engaged in evening worship, and sweet melodies floated upon the evening air. Thus the promise finds fulfilment: "The wilderness and the solitary place shall be glad for them; and the desert shall rejoice and blossom as the rose. It shall blossom abundantly, and rejoice even with joy and singing."

An attempt was made in 1875 to reach the debased and cannibal savages of New Britain and New Ireland. The principal agents in the enterprise, in addition to an intrepid English missionary and his noble wife, were earnest Fijian and Samoan converts. Natives of the South Sea have generally considerable force of character, and when brought thoroughly under the influence of the gospel are ready for pioneer service. "By the blessing of God," writes Professor Geden, "upon untold labor and suffering, the ancient triumphs of the cross have been repeated in these long neglected groups of the Pacific Islands; and, at this time, only seven years from the first landing on them of Christian missionaries, it is not too much to say that the old evil things are passing away, and that all things promise to become new. Many of the people, by an evangelical conversion that would have made the hearts of St. Paul and St. John to leap for joy, have been turned from darkness to light."*

Equally signal has been the success of the London Society's mission to numerous islands of the Torres Straits. At Saibai and Dauan the natives are clothed; for in the South Sea the wearing of suitable apparel is regarded as the badge of Christianity—an outward and visible sign of an inward and spiritual grace.

Apparently one of the most hopeless schemes of the Christian Church was the attempt to evangelize the aborigines of Australia. Once the Papuans had that great territory in possession; but now, numbering only some thirty or forty thousand, they form an insignificant element of the expanding southern population. Beyond comparison even with Esquimaux and Bushmen, the natives of Australia are at the lowest level of degraded humanity. Their language has no equivalent for such words as faith and forgiveness, truth and honesty. A vague notion of a good and evil spirit exists among them; but no religion, not even that of idol worship. Low and loathsome in habit and appetite, it is scarcely a matter of surprise that even Christian people were dubious as to the result of efforts for their material and moral improvement.† But the gospel is the power of God unto sal-

---

* London *Methodist Recorder*, November, 1882.

† A brother of the writer, by whom features of the work have been described, is at present the Secretary of an Australian Association for the Improvement of the Aborigines.

vation to every one that believeth. Divine grace has touched and roused even the long-dormant faculties of the Papuan. Under the influence of Christian teaching, accompanied by the energy of the Holy Ghost, latent forces have been developed. When the Moravian Bishop De Schweinitz looked at the photograph of one of the earliest converts, an assistant at the Ebenezer Mission, and heard of the fervor of his prayer and the impressiveness of his sermons, he "could scarcely believe that this man had been a naked savage, squatting in the sand and roasting lizards for his food, joining his countrymen in the vilest abominations, and living as near to the state of the irrational creation as it is possible for a human being to reach." *

The signal triumphs of the gospel, in the lands of uncivilized heathenism, demonstrate a continued efficacy and an abiding adaptation to all the variations and conditions of the human race. It purifies and consecrates the highest culture, and it also elevates and blesses the most deeply-sunken tribes of earth.

A characteristic sermon, on the general spread of the gospel, was preached by an eminent evangelist of the last century. An attempt was made to trace out the probable course of spiritual effort and influence, and of the conversion of the world to Christ. It was supposed that the heathen bordering on the frontier lines of Christendom would be the first to be led to worship

---

* *Evangelical Alliance*, 1873, p. 621.

God in spirit and in truth. The God of love would then prepare a pathway for His messengers into the polar regions, the deepest recesses of America, the interior parts of Africa, "yea, into the heart of China and Japan, with the countries adjoining them." But one "considerable difficulty" still remained. There were uncivilized people beyond the range of commercial enterprise, and apparently inaccessible to the missionaries of the cross. "Such are the inhabitants of the numerous islands of the South Sea, and probably in all the larger branches of the ocean. Now, what shall be done for these outcasts of men?"* The Polynesian and other groups of islanders in the Southern Pacific had an evil reputation. They were distant from the abodes of civilization. Such was the active ferocity of their nature, and the debasing character of their customs and superstitions, that the venerable preacher concluded they would be the last of all the dwellers of the earth to receive the gospel. But yet, in those dark and distant isles of the ocean, missionary enterprise has won its brightest wreath, and Christianity has chronicled some of its most magnificent triumphs.

The people of the Pacific Islands, as they have experienced the regenerating power of the gospel, have made amazing bounds in the direction of cultured manners, remunerative industries, interchange of com-

---

* *Wesley's Sermons*, Vol. VI. of Works, p. 286.

modities, and the arts and amenities of national and social life.

> "The voice of the world shouts its chorus,
> Its pæan for those who have won."

And shall we not express our gratitude for missionary achievement and progress? If apart from the power of the cross, the processes of civilization had proved equally potent and successful for the amelioration of the human race, would not the world have rung with plaudits? Had merely ethical inculcation softened and subdued the barbarities and ferocities of cannibal tribes, might not eloquence have pronounced its glowing eulogiums? If an anthropological scheme and policy had been productive of such beautiful and beneficent results, what garlands would have been woven for the promoters of the enterprise! The heroic men who have formed the vanguard of the missions may not win or wear the distinctions of earth, but they share in the exultation of the Apostle: "Now thanks be unto God, which always causeth us to triumph in Christ, and maketh manifest the savor of His knowledge by us in every place."*

---

* It has been mainly through the light of missionary agency that the miseries of uncivilized heathenism have come to be understood; and, hence, in previous pages, there has been repeated reference to pioneer enterprise. The *present aspect* of missions will form the subject of a subsequent section.

"Scarcely any one man has a clear conception of the internal operations of the numerous Societies in the Old and New Worlds, in Africa, Australia, and the South Seas. Many know much about this or that field, some are familiar with several fields, but no one comprehends them all: the materials of knowledge are scattered through hundreds of periodicals, and the statistics change with almost every mail."—*Prof. Christlieb.*

V.

MODERN MISSIONS AND MISSION STATIONS.

WHAT of modern Protestant missions? To what extent has the Church of Christ, in fulfilment of hallowed obligation, responded to the world-wide Macedonian appeal? How did this evangelical movement originate? What societies have been organized by the leading denominations? What mission stations are at present occupied, and in what force? What are the most important tabulations, and what special successes have been chronicled? In answer to numerous questions, an attempt may be made to summarise a few main historic facts, and to make the circuit of mission stations.

Modern missions, now expanding into proportions of great magnitude, belong largely to the present century. It is interesting, however, to trace back to an earlier date the development of a missionary spirit. Perhaps the first attempts at Protestant propaganda were a Swedish mission to Lapland and an arbitrary effort of Dutch cinnamon traders to convert the Buddhists of Ceylon to a profession of the faith of Christ. In 1634, Robert Junius began a temporarily successful mission to the island of Formosa. The interesting mission of John Eliot to the Indians of Massachusetts, into whose language the New Testament was translated, the precursor of numerous missionary versions, was commenced in 1646. New-England colonists were deeply imbued with the idea of converting the heathen tribes of the continent. "The propagating the gospel," wrote the founders of Salem, " is the one thing we do profess above all to be our aim in settling this plantation." An early State seal of Massachusetts bore for its motto the Macedonian cry: " Come over and help us." The religious enthusiasm which marked the period of the Commonwealth in England was productive of missionary spirit and purpose. On July 27th, 1648, an ordinance passed in Parliament to constitute a "Society for the Propagation of the Gospel in New England." According to the recital of the preamble to that missionary measure, "the Commons of England assembled in Parliament, having received intelligence that the heathen of New England were beginning to call on the name of the Lord, felt bound to assist in such a work." One of Oliver Cromwell's proposed measures for the promotion of the Protestant religion, that might have been carried into effect had his life been spared a few years longer, was the formation of a *Congregatio de Propaganda Fide*, with secretaries paid by State, and the Chelsea College fitted up for its reception.

The present "Society for the Propagation of the Gospel in Foreign Parts," organized in 1701, intended chiefly for the benefit of colonists, was an outcome of Puritan Parliamentary deliberations. A Danish mission to Southern India was commenced in 1705;

founded by noble men, Ziegenbalg and Plutcho, followed by the apostolic Schwartz. Full for a time of bright promise, that Halle-Danish mission was paralyzed by German rationalism, and its glory departed. Hans Egede, of Denmark, having read scanty accounts of Greenlanders and their hardships amid the Arctic frosts, was roused to an enthusiastic interest for their spiritual welfare, and determined to brave the discomforts of polar life. The Greenland mission was begun in 1721.

Moravian missions, so nobly signalized, date from 1732. Under the direction of Count Zinzendorf, a number of Protestant exiles gathered at New Hernhutt, and were educated for evangelical enterprise. When the community numbered only six hundred persons, they began the first mission beyond the sea, and five months later a second missionary sailed to a foreign shore. From "the Lord's Watch," to those that needed them most, there went out a succession of faithful messengers of salvation. Within five years as many missions were founded. In spite of heat and cold, ministering to slaves in the West Indies and to Hottentots in South Africa, seeking a home among the ice-bound fiords of the hard and dreary Greenland coast, most forbidding fields of labor were selected.

> "Fired with a zeal peculiar, they defy
> The rage and rigor of a polar sky,
> And plant successfully sweet Sharon's rose
> On icy plains, and in eternal snows."

Moravians have recently celebrated their 150th missionary anniversary; and, with exceedingly limited resources, out of their munificence of spirit and the abounding of liberality, they now sustain three hundred and fifteen missionaries in the foreign field. "The missionary thought," says Dr. Thompson, "grew with their growth; it had a conspicuous place in all their plans and movements; it is the staple of their literature; it was prophetically symbolized in the ancient Episcopal seal of their Church—on a crimson ground—a lamb bearing the resurrection cross, from which hangs a triumphant banner, with the motto: *Vicit agnus noster; eum sequamur:* (Our Lamb has conquered: Him let us follow)."

In 1784 the distinguished pioneer of Wesleyan missions, Rev. Dr. Coke, made the first of his sixteen Atlantic voyages. Fired with the idea of a universal evangelization, he longed for the wings of an angel and the voice of a trumpet, that he might proclaim the gospel east and west, north and south. On Christmas morning, 1786, the flaming evangelist landed on the shores of Antigua, and began a gloriously successful mission to the negroes of the West Indies. To the last the missionary fire of Coke knew no abatement, and he found a grave in the depth of an Eastern sea, on the way to India.*

The Baptist Association which met at Nottingham in June, 1792, was signalized by a memorable and now

---

*The work of Wesleyan missionary enterprise, for more than a double decade under the immediate charge of Dr. Coke, was more fully organized by the formation of a society in 1813.

historic missionary sermon. The preacher was William Carey. An inspiring passage was read from Isaiah: "Enlarge the place of thy tent, and let them stretch forth the curtains of thine habitations: spare not, lengthen thy cords, and strengthen thy stakes; for thou shalt break forth on the right hand and on the left; and thy seed shall inherit the Gentiles, and make the desolate cities to be inhabited." They must expect great things from God, and attempt great things for God. A genuine missionary fire blazed out in the sermon. The enthusiasm was contagious, and led to grand results. On the 2nd of October, in the parlor of Mrs. Wallis, at Kettering, Northamptonshire, a handful of Baptist ministers met to devise means for the world's conversion. It was a day of small and feeble things. The faith of the men was sublime. A Missionary Society was formed that day, and the year following, 1793, the first missionaries sailed for India. On his way out to the East, still fired with the expanding idea of missionary enterprise, Carey sent back an earnest appeal to the people at home. Aspirations were not bounded by the necessities of India, or even of all Asia. Africa was but a little way from England, and Madagascar a little further on. South America and the numerous and large islands in the India and China Seas would not, he hoped, be passed over.

At a meeting of the Independent or Congregational ministers, held at Warwick, June 29th, 1793, a missionary question was proposed for consideration:

"What is the duty of Christians with respect to the spread of the gospel?" It was felt to be a solemn obligation "to employ every means in their power to spread the knowledge of the gospel both at home and abroad." A resolution was adopted in favor of the organization of a Missionary Union, and it was decided that the first Monday evening of each month should be set apart for prayer for the success of all denominations in their attempts to spread abroad the knowledge of salvation. Two years later, 1795, in furtherance of the same views, the London Missionary Society was founded; composed at first of members of several evangelical communities, it was soon left to the management of the Independents. Under the leadership of Simeon of Cambridge, Venn, and others, the Church Missionary Society was established in 1799. In 1804 a few Christian men came together in a London business office to devise means for giving the Bible to destitute parts of Wales. But why not for the world? Born of that sudden inspiration, the British and Foreign Bible Society was at once organized.

The enterprise of the Church has at different times been directed towards God's ancient people. There has been the longing of many a heart, "O that the salvation of Israel were come out of Zion!" This feeling has found practical expression in the organization of several societies: the London Society for Promoting Christianity among the Jews in 1808, the Church of Scotland Society in 1840, the British

Society in 1842, the Mission of the Free Church of Scotland in 1843, and other societies. A measure of success has attended these laudable efforts. One hundred thousand Jews have been baptized into the faith of Christ. But have Christians on the whole been sufficiently solicitous for the salvation of all Israel? "To the Jew first" was the apostolic idea of spiritual enterprise. Are not many bright hopes and anticipations bound up with the fortunes and promised restoration of the covenant race? "Now, if the fall of them be the riches of the world, and the diminishing of them the riches of the Gentiles, how much more their fulness?"

A movement among the students of a New England seminary led to the organization of the first missionary society on the American continent. The saintly mother of Samuel I. Mills had early dedicated him to God; and, when converted, his thoughts turned to missions. One day, as several of the students met to hold a prayer-meeting in a neighboring grove, a thunder-storm drove them to the shelter of a haystack. There the question of missions was discussed. The gospel ought to be at once sent, through some of their own number, to the dark heathen of Asia. This matter became the subject of earnest prayer. A marble shaft crowns the historic spot. But the resolve of that band of five students found a more enduring memorial. It led to the formation, June, 1810, of the American Board of Foreign Missions—a society which has sent out well-nigh two thousand missionaries; whose agents have reduced to writing no less than twenty-six different languages, and made numerous translations of the Scriptures, the laborers of which have been signally successful in the work of conversion, and have "raised nations from the lowest forms of heathenism to Christian civilization."

The earlier history of the modern mission movement—the daring and splendid programme adopted, the conspicuously inadequate means at the disposal of the promoters of the enterprise, and the sublime faith and heroic fortitude of the missionary pioneer—forms a theme of almost unrivalled interest. "There are few things in human history that wear an aspect of higher moral grandeur than the opening of what are now our great missions. Among the glories of the century is none greater than this."* Bare statement conveys but little idea of actual expansion. Feeble and fluctuating efforts have grown up into strong and systematized action. Each succeeding decade has shown continuous progress. Seven societies have been multiplied to seventy. Instead of the faint glimmer of a few struggling missions, scarcely relieving the darkness of heathenism, the light of twenty thousand stations stream out upon the earth.

> "On mountain tops the watch-fires glow,
> Where scattered wide the watchmen stand;
> Voice echoes voice, and onward flow
> The joyous shouts from every land."

---

* *The 19th Century*, by Robert Mackenzie, Frank. Sq. Ed., p. 38.

In order to obtain an adequate impression of missionary enterprise, in its truly magnificent proportions, it is necessary to glance over the entire field of operations. A visit to the principal stations takes us round the world. Ten years ago the missions of the Methodist Episcopal Church were "the travel posts" by which a missionary statesman and his companions made the circuit of the globe. Westward from New York, they crossed the continent, halting for a brief space at the Mongolian mission on the Pacific Coast. An ocean voyage brought them to Japan, affording intercourse with the brethren at Yokohama and Jeddo; thence to China, and the missions at Foo-Chow, Kukiang and Peking; thence westward to India, Turkey, and home; "still facing the setting sun, journeying by the signal fires of mission stations, and to the minstrelsy of mission songs."

Taking Canada as a geographical centre and starting-point in our missionary outlook, a field of stern toil lies to the north; for men have braved and borne the snows of Labrador and the rigors of the frozen zone. Greenland's icy mountains have been celebrated in story and song as the scene of inevitable hardships and of indomitable zeal. That enterprise was the morning star of the modern movement. It is nearly a century and a half since the brave Scandinavian, Egede, accompanied by his not less heroic wife, left a little Fatherland parish and sought the stormy and frost-bound regions of the Arctic. Faith and patience were long and sorely tested by the stupidity of the natives. But at last there came a memorable day, when torpid sensibilities were touched, a fountain of feeling unsealed, and the success of the mission assured. The work remains to this day. Greenland has seventy missionaries, and a Christian community of twelve thousand people.

The missions of North America generally, through all their history and across the continent, have been signalized by deeds of intrepidity and heroism. No work could be more arduous than that of reaching the roaming tribes of the Great Lone Land, in their pagan hardness. But, at an early period, wherever the Hudson's Bay Company established its "storm-beaten stations," James Evans and other pioneers drove their dog sledges, and the trading posts became centres of religious influence. The work is still perpetuated by men of like consecrated character and purpose. John McDougall emulates the spirit and treads in the steps of his sainted and immortal father. The mission of Thomas Crosby to the Indians of British Columbia, like a pillar of fire suddenly kindled in a dark place, brightens a long line of Pacific coast, and claims the attention of wandering heathen tribes. Dr. Sheldon Jackson is known beyond the limits of his vast charge as "the apostle of the Rocky Mountains."

The great southern field has had less of the romance of missions than some other sections of this American continent. But the present outlook is full of hopeful interest. Missionaries are making good their position in Mexico. That country was entered fourteen years ago. Eight Protestant societies, with one hundred and fifty agents, now report ten thousand converts, from a mass of ten million of spiritually degraded people. Trade has recently received an immense impetus; and, side by side with the revival of commerce, through beautiful Mexican valleys, "the streams of salvation are already flowing in deeper and swifter currents."

The prevailing religion of Central America, with its several miniature republics, comprising an aggregate population of two million and seven hundred thousand, is that of Roman Catholicism. An English Wesleyan mission has been sustained for several years at Honduras. The Moravians have seven stations along the Musquito coast, and over a thousand members. A gracious revival of religion has been experienced during the past year and several hundred members added to the communion.

There are few lands of sunnier or richer tropical beauty than those of the West India Isles. But at the commencement of the century the world had scarcely a fouler spot. Society was fetid with crime; "a black amalgam of European and African vices, combining the grossness of the one with the fire of the other." Missions were an experiment. The men who led the van bore in their bodies the marks of the Lord Jesus. But as the facts of slavery and of social life came to be known, the heart and conscience of England were aroused. Voices were heard across the deep. A signal flame was seen to burn beneath a darkened sky. Eloquent men demanded that the shackles should be struck off from the slave, and that through religious instruction some reparation should be made for long-continued and grievous wrong. Since then those islands have been brought under the influence of Christianity, and can scarcely be regarded now as missions in the proper sense. A new history has been begun. Three hundred ministers of several denominations report "eighty-five thousand communicants, and two hundred and fifty thousand regular attendants at the house of God." It is somewhat disappointing to notice, in a cruise through the archipelago, that pulpits are generally occupied by foreign preachers. Have the ranks of West India converts failed to furnish suitable material for a native ministry?

As we touch the continent, an Indian mission of British Guiana, begun forty years ago, sends a gleam of light across the waves. A missionary of the Propagation Society, in the early part of 1881, baptized fourteen hundred natives; and he believes that there are few cases, "where so many at a time, with so little to tempt them, have sought admission into the Christian Church." The Moravians began their work at Paramaribo over a century ago. They have a strong station, thousands of adherents, and are responding to an earnest appeal from the Bushland.

A magnificent territory almost as large as Europe, with a population of eleven million, forms the empire of Brazil. The hope has long been cherished, as the result of closer contact with Protestant civilization and commerce, that a brighter and better era would be inaugurated in the religious life of that land. But Romanism dominates here in its most intolerant and superstitious form, and certainly the Papal Church has little reason to be proud of its spiritual achievements.

"Pray for South America!" Such was the request recently forwarded to the monthly prayer concert of one of the great missionary Churches. The spiritual destitution of nine republics and ten nations were touchingly described; their hopeless moral condition calling to the keepers of God's oracles with the Macedonian voice: *Come over and help us.* Missions on the Brazilian coast, at Montevideo and Buenos Ayres on the Plata shores, at Rosario in the interior, and at a few points on the West Coast, are still few and far between; and yet "from these centres the lines must go out to evangelize the continent." The Brazilian work is carried on under the auspices of Presbyterians, Congregationalists, and Southern Methodists. Missionaries of the Northern Methodist Church are said to be doing an excellent work in the South-Eastern republics. Presbyterians and Congregationalists are planting their stations along the West Coast, and there Dr. William Taylor is working out a great experiment in the line of a Pauline method. The South American Missionary Society has given the gospel to Patagonia, at the extremity of the continent, to the Falkland Islands, and to Terra del Fuego. The exclamation of

Humbolt's guides, as—from the beautiful constellation of the Southern Cross, which sets the sign of our redemption in the heavens—they noted the morning hour, finds application in a spiritual sense to the nations of South America: "*Midnight is past: the Cross bends!*"

From the continent we take our course to the island world of the Pacific. Polynesia, *many* islands, set like gems in the crystal sea, presents a scene of unique beauty, and of rare missionary interest. A century has witnessed marvellous changes. When first discovered, and made known to the civilized world, darkness and barbarism everywhere prevailed. The people were savage, superstitious, and grossly vile. But the power of the gospel has there been gloriously exhibited. What thrilling and triumphant memories are associated with such names as Tonga and Tahiti, Samoan and Society Isles! "In more than three hundred islands of eastern and southern Polynesia," says Dr. Mullens, "the gospel has swept heathenism entirely away." Former dark rites are now no longer practised. Heathen legends have vanished. Tribal wars have ceased. Songs of the cannibal feast have given place to the sweet strains of the Redeemer's praise. Fields are cultivated. Commerce prospers. Law is recognized. Native Churches are generously supported. "The work of missions may be said to be practically over."

Sixty years ago, Tonga had not a single convert to the faith of Christ. Three missionaries of the London

Society, who first made the attempt to reclaim the fierce savages, were murdered. But there is scarcely a vestige of heathenism now left in that group.

The islands of Fiji, as we have seen, were inhabited by a race of ferocious cannibals; but, through a marvellously successful Christian agency, twenty-five thousand of these natives have been enrolled as communicants of the Wesleyan Church, and one hundred thousand assemble regularly for public worship. "You pass from isle to isle," under the intelligent guidance of Miss Gordon Cumming, "certain everywhere to find the same cordial reception from women and men. Every village in the eighty islands has built for itself a church, and a house for the native teacher or preacher. Can you realize that *there are more than nine thousand Wesleyan churches in Fiji*, at every one of which the services are crowded by devout congregations; and that the first sound that greets your ear at dawn, and the last at night, is that of hymn-singing rising from each dwelling at the hour of morning and evening worship."

To the north-west of Fiji are the New Hebrides, a mission field of the Presbyterian Church of Nova Scotia; where on the blood-stained island of Eromanga the immortal John Williams and the Gordons of these Provinces were martyred. At Aneityam a marble tablet has been inscribed to the memory of Rev. John Geddie: "When he landed in 1848, there were no Christians here; and when he left, 1872, there were no heathens." The vivid description of this missionary's first experience in his selected field will long be remembered by Nova Scotia audiences. A cannibal chief, afterwards converted to God, lurked around his hut on the night of his arrival. The savage was intent upon murderous purpose. But a power which he could not understand, and which was felt to be as a strange spell, restrained his hand; "and there," said the missionary, producing a polished battle-axe, "is the weapon with which he intended to perpetrate the deed." Further to the north, on the island of Nukapu, of the Swallow group, a great missionary bishop of the Church of England, John Coleridge Patteson, met a martyr's death in 1871.

Crossing the equator, leaving Micronesia on the left, we halt at the Sandwich Islands, where Captain Cook was murdered in 1779. Hawaiians were formerly heathens of a low and disgusting type. Abominable vices and habits were tending to national deterioration, and to a rapid diminution of population. Such was the condition of the Sandwich Islands, when, in 1719, a small missionary party sailed from Boston for the purpose of bringing the inhabitants under the influence of Christianity. The patient faith and persistent purpose of the men and women who fulfilled that mission claim a permanent record. Success was equal to the most sanguine anticipation. Civilization was introduced. The people were christianized. Churches became self-supporting, both in regard to men and means. Native ministers were ordained to the pastorate of influential congregations. This was the work of fifty years. The mission has closed, having been struck off from the roll of the American Board. The entire cost of turning this little nation from idols to serve the living God was "greatly less than half the cost of one iron-clad ship of war," less than half the annual value of the country's increasing commerce. Hawaii has the banner church of the Protestant world, numbering between four and five thousand communicants. A jubilee sermon, June 1870, in memorial of deliverance from heathenism and the introduction of Christianity, was preached by a native pastor. It would be pleasant to linger on these isles of the ocean, where a nation has been born in our day. But we have many stations to visit, and must embark for "the Land of the Rising Sun."

The favored empire of Japan, in which we begin to meet and mingle with the forms of Oriental life, is the newest field of modern missions. The first missionaries to enter the country, after the unlocking of treaty ports, were those of the Protestant Episcopal, Presbyterian and Reformed Churches of America, in 1859. An exceedingly effective and successful work was organized by the American Board in 1869. Contingents were furnished by the Methodist Episcopal Church of the United States in 1873, and also by the Methodist Church of Canada. "We entered Japan," says Dr. Cochran, "just as the time was ripe for Christian work."* Twenty different societies are

---

* The main facts connected with the opening of Japan are tersely summarized, by Dr. George Cochran, in papers furnished for the *Canadian Methodist Magazine*, December, 1880, and *The Missionary Outlook*, January, 1883.

laboring harmoniously together in this land of the morning, for the evangelization of thirty-five million of people. A public service was held in Tokio, April 1880, at which fourteen societies were represented, to celebrate the consummation of a complete translation of the New Testament into the Japanese language. The aggregate statistics of missions, as published in the report of the Evangelical Alliance of Japan, for 1882, comprise one hundred and forty-five missionaries, one hundred and forty-nine ordained and assistant preachers, seventy-one theological students, and nearly five thousand communicants. The week of prayer at the commencement of 1883, was followed by a very blessed outpouring of the Holy Spirit, resulting in a more rapid accession of converts than had been previously known. An open Bible and a Pentecostal baptism are Japan's best hope. Yes, the day breaketh!

Corea, "the Land of Morning Calm," to the west of Japan, with a population of ten million, intense adherents of Confucius, is slow to open her gates to the messengers of salvation. There is no missionary station to attract us to the shores of that peninsula, and we pass on to the vast and populous empire lying on the south-eastern slope of the Asiatic continent; an immense territory, numbering over seventeen hundred walled cities, and an estimated population of nearly four hundred million.

A great and growing work is being done for China. Four hundred missionaries, including physicians and ladies, are fulfilling a blessed ministry, and are extending their efforts to the interior of the provinces. It took ten years to increase the first ten converts to a force of two hundred and twenty. But during half a decade, from 1877, communicants have increased from thirteen to twenty thousand. Between three and four hundred schools have been established, and other agencies are employed for diffusing gospel light. Professor Legge, of Oxford, claims that in thirty-five years Chinese converts have been multiplied two thousand-fold, the rate of increase being greater year by year. "Suppose it to continue the same other thirty-five years, and in 1913 there will be thirty-six millions of communicants, and a professedly Christian population of one hundred millions." Such statistical studies and estimates have a certain value. They have a basis of ascertained fact. But the most essential laws and forces of spiritual dynamics are not to be measured or tabulated. The residue of the Spirit is with God. China shall be visited with a Divine glory.

Glancing away to the adjacent island of Formosa, with its three or four million of people, the light of a noble and successful mission gladdens the vision. Twelve years ago, one Saturday afternoon, without any knowledge of the language, a missionary of the Presbyterian Church of Canada, Dr. McKay, landed on the Formosan coast. What a moving tale of toil, trial, and triumph he has now to recite! After four months he began to preach in a new and difficult tongue, and five months later a native convert accompanied him on a missionary tour. Other converts were won. Fierce persecution had to be encountered. Martyrs died for the truth. Savages clamored for the blood of the intrepid missionary, but he seemed to be shielded by an invisible power. The son of a chief and four others were shot and decapitated; and over their graves Dr. McKay inscribed a monumental stone, "Blessed are the dead which die in the Lord." Still the word of the Lord grew and prevailed. Twenty churches have been planted in the northern part of the island, and as many native preachers have been raised up to make known the gospel to their countrymen.

The Asiatic coast line brings us to an important peninsula lying between China and India. It comprises Siam and Burmah, with their connected territory, and a population of some fifteen million. Siam, "the Kingdom of the Free," receptive of Western ideas, has yet to know the truth which can really secure the highest freedom. Buddhism is there enthroned, and its splendid temples are sustained at an annual cost of twenty-five million of dollars. Missionaries of the Presbyterian Board bear the banner of evangelical enterprise in Siam. "Come, Lord Jesus, come quickly," is the prayer of a Laos missionary's devoted wife, "reveal Thyself to those poor benighted ones." The work of the Baptist missionaries in Burmah has won wide and well-deserved renown. The names of the sainted Judson and his gifted wives " will be remembered in the churches of Burmah in future times, when the pagodas of Guatama shall have fallen, and the spires of Christian temples shall gleam along the waters of the Irawaddy and Salwen."

MISSION STATIONS. 139

From the peninsula we pass on to the islands of the Indian Archipelago, Sumatra, populous Java, spacious Borneo, and the deep bays of Celebes, with a population of nearly thirty million. The Mohammedan religion very largely obtains; but there are exceptions, as in the Buddhism of the Philippine group. Propagation and Dutch societies have stations at Sumatra. Thirty Dutch missionaries seek to establish the Reformed faith in Java. Rhenish societies have made a beginning in Borneo. Celebes is said to be the most prosperous mission of the Holland Churches, having important stations and thousands of converts among the Malays of the peninsula. But up to the present time the strength of evangelical forces is palpably and painfully inadequate to the great work of bringing those beautiful islands beneath the benign influence of the gospel of Christ.

New Guinea, to the east of the archipelago, is inhabited by a Papuan race of people. It is one of the largest islands on the globe, and probably one of the darkest spots of heathendom. Not much was really known of the place or the people until the missionaries of the London Society planned their campaign about ten years ago; except that the climate was deadly, the tribes savage and degraded, and the coast one that seamen sought to avoid. But courageous missionary exploration has won the high encomium and medal of the Royal Geographical Society, and has led to the discovery of a superior type of people—in the interior. Already strong stations have been planted along the line of immense coast, and the gospel will doubtless follow rapidly in the direction of recent exploration.

The great insular continent of Australia, to which in geographical order we next arrive, is the home of three million of enterprising people, destined at no distant period to the possession of a mighty population. At the commencement of this century, in common with Tasmania, New Zealand, and adjacent islands, it was engulfed in deepest night. The country was little noticed except as a penal colony. No one dreamed that in so short a period it was to become the scene of a prosperous commerce; bound to the rest of the civilized world by rapid and continuous communication, lines of superb steamers, and fleets of sailing ships. The first record concerning the heroic pioneer of Wesleyan missions, Samuel Leigh, was to the effect that he had sailed for Australia eighteen months before, and had not been heard from. Australian Christianity, as represented by the leading evangelical denominations, exhibits a commanding character, having thoroughly organized agencies and institutions, and numerous missions to surrounding groups of islands. There is said to be "a larger proportion of well-educated people in the Australian colonies than among the same number of people at home, and their religious feeling is fully equal."*

A pleasant sail over an equatorial sea, fanned by

---

* *Statistics of Protestant Missionary Societies*, 1872, p. 96.

breezes from spicy isles, takes us to the coral strand of Ceylon, "the celebrated Taprobane of other ages." Were it not for the exhibitions of human depravity, this sunny and voluptuous island might be regarded as a paradise; but the exquisite beauty of scenery must not render us insensible to the vileness of man, and the need of regenerating energy. Ceylon was early selected as a missionary field. Episcopal and Wesleyan societies are doing a strong and successful work.

Thought turns eagerly to India. That great southern Asiatic peninsula may well be regarded as the Thermopylæ of modern missions. "India won," said the late Bishop Thompson, "and Asia is saved." This magnificent territory extends from Burmah to the distant Indus, and from Ceylon to Cashmere, a distance of two thousand miles. There is very much land to be possessed. An immense population, one-sixth of the human race, chiefly owns the supremacy of Queen Victoria, and has a special claim upon the thought and sympathies of British Christians. Earlier contingents of the missionary army forced their way in the face of all but insuperable obstacles. But there has been a visible interposition of Providence in behalf of the cause of India's evangelization. Conditions have hopefully changed. The Churches have not been slow to acknowledge the hand of God as it was "seen over against them," or to take advantage of new and auspicious openings for the spread of the gospel. Twenty-eight societies, represented by over a thousand missionaries, are moving in the harmony and vigor of concerted and aggressive action. Up to the close of the first half of this century, 1851, there were only about ninety thousand Christians in Hindustan; but an aggregate of nearly half a million is now reported, one-third of whom are communicants.* Each period exhibits an increasing momentum of missionary effort. Two facts challenge special attention. Returns for the decade ending December, 1881, reveal the hopeful fact that in these ten years the number of converts and of native ministers has been doubled. "None of the European or American Churches can exhibit such an increase." The Anglican Mission at Tinnevelly continues to be signalized by its accessions of converts. During the year 1882, one thousand and eight hundred persons were baptized, upon the profession of their faith, by the Rev. I. S. Clough, of the Baptist Telugu Mission. Five hundred natives, in a body, have lately applied for baptism at a Wesleyan station in the Madras Presidency. The second Decennial Conference, composed of missionaries from every part of

---

* *The Gospel in all Lands*, February, 1883.

* Statistics, prepared for the Calcutta Decennial Conference, indicate the increase of the decade:

NATIVE CHRISTIANS.			COMMUNICANTS.		
	1871.	1881.		1871.	1881.
India	224,258	417,372	India	52,816	113,325
Burmah	62,720	75,510	Burmah	20,514	24,929
Ceylon	31,376	35,708	Ceylon	5,164	6,843
Total	318,363	528,590	Total	78,494	145,097

India, was held at Calcutta early in January, 1883. Thanks were offered to God for the unparalleled success which had crowned the toilers in that land. "That which in popular phrase is called evangelical Christianity," wrote an observer of the assembly gathered on the banks of the Hooghly, "is a mighty power in the Empire, full of vitality and energy, intensely aggressive, organized and equipped for victory, and on the march to the goal of certain success." *

From India the pioneer missionary has crossed the border line to Afghanistan. Four millions of Afghans, though claiming a descent from the ten tribes of Israel, are followers of the Arabian prophet. The Church of England station at Peshawur has a membership of ninety converted Mohammedans. A noble boon to the Afghan is the Pushtu translation of the New Testament; forming, as in many other cases, the foundation of a Christian literature. The conversion of a notorious robber, Dilawar Khan, on whose head the British had set a price, furnished a striking illustration of the transforming power of the gospel, and of the influence of genuine Christian character. Two hundred of the Moslem population are said to have been "led by him, at least intellectually, to renounce the faith of Islam, and to accept the teachings of God's word."

The light of the Persian sky has faded. No longer

---

* *India Witness*, January 6th, 1883.

do the wise men from the East bring their offerings of gold and frankincense and myrrh to the shrine of the world's Redeemer. The cold Crescent, not the star of Bethlehem, "the bright and morning star," shines over the land of the Sophi. The population of four and a half million, though mostly Moslem, includes a few Jews, and about 70,000 Armenians and Nestorians. Missionaries of the Church of England follow in the labours of the saintly Henry Martyn, whose name and memory are imperishably associated with missionary enterprise in that Eastern field. The strong missions of Persia are those of the American Presbyterian Church. They have recently been favored with a gracious revival, in which some Jews and many Nestorians have been brought to a knowledge of the Saviour. Translations of the Word of God bring within the reach of all the people of Persia a treasure more precious than the pearls of Ormuz.

The great Arabian peninsula, with a population of some nine millions, extends from the Persian Gulf to the Red Sea, and from the Gulf of Aden to the borders of Syria, on the Mediterranean. The Arabian people, endowed with intellectual qualities of a high order, full of force and fire, were first to accept and to propagate the creed of the Koran. To them "Mohammed delivered the scymeter, as the instrument of his apostolate," and the rapid success of the new faith must have been in a great measure due to the splendid qualities of the Arab race. When shall the fiery children of the desert be won to the Redeemer's cross?

The Bible has been rendered into the flexible Arabic, the sacred language of Islam, "an accurate and elegant version." Otherwise little is being done to promote a purer faith:

> "See where o'er desert wastes they err,
> And neither food nor feeder have,
> Nor fold, nor place of refuge near,
> For no man cares their souls to save."

In Asiatic Turkey, where there is much to detain us, and where a great work has been begun, a very different state of things obtains. The dominant religion is Mohammedanism. But the population of sixteen million includes numerous communities of Christians. Turkey in Asia comprises lands of sacred interest: Mesopotamia and Armenia, Bashan and Palestine, Syria and Asia Minor; the sites of Nineveh and Babylon, the mountains of Ararat and Lebanon, and the ancient cities of Damascus and Jerusalem. The Holy Land is still defiled and degraded by the tyrannies of the Moslem. The hoof of the Turk is said to wither every green thing, and nowhere else has the invader left a more desolate track than in the Lord's land. Missionary work has at different times been prosecuted with a good deal of enthusiasm among the Jews of Palestine. Many faithful laborers have gone forth weeping, bearing precious seed. The Church of England has a bishop resident on Mount Zion, and mission stations at Jerusalem, Jaffa, Nablous, Nazareth, Gaza, and ancient Ramoth Gilead. But the promised day of Israel does not seem yet to have come. The

Jews are still a scattered people, and in some lands the bitterness of exile knows but little abatement. The pathetic lament of the Hebrew prophet, calling for pity and help at the time of the captivity, is still the Macedonian cry of the daughter of Judah, as she weeps beneath the palm tree: "Is it nothing to you all ye that pass by? Behold and see if there be any sorrow like unto my sorrow?"

Amidst scenes and surroundings of Bible interest, the missionaries of the American Board have made for themselves a noble record, and have challenged the admiration of every section of the Christian Church. For several years the work, which has now expanded into proportions of magnitude and importance, has been prosecuted at an annual expenditure of $150,000. The mission has a force of fifty-four ministers sent out from home, fifty-seven native ordained preachers, nearly one hundred lady missionaries, and some five hundred other helpers in various departments of evangelistic and educational enterprise. A line of stations stretches from the boundaries of Persia to the banks of the Bosphorus, on to Bulgaria south of the Balkans, and from Orontes and Aleppo to the borders of the Black Sea. Through translation of the Bible, a great work has been done for Western Asia. An eminent living missionary has taken part in the preparation of Armenian, Armeno-Turkish, and Bulgarian versions. The Word of God has been given to a large portion of the Ottoman empire. On the banks of the Nile, throughout the deserts of Arabia, by the rivers of

Babylon, at Ur of the Chaldees, in the land of Gennesaret, amongst the ruins of the Seven Churches of Asia, the sacred Scriptures have been unsealed, and can be read by the people in their own tongue.

Oriental Churches scattered over a wide region must always excite a deep interest. Christian sects exist in the very heart of great Moslem communities. Armenian, Nestorian, Copt, and especially Greek, Churches are found in Persia, Turkey, Egypt, and Syria; in such cities and centres as Aleppo and Damascus, Cairo and Constantinople. In spite of Mohammedan hate and determined attempts at proselytism, numerous communities have maintained for centuries a struggling life and organization. Although exhibiting an inferior type of Christianity, such sects bear a sacred name, maintain some forms of spiritual worship, and are the depositaries of revealed truth. To Mussulmans they represent the religion of the New Testament. Hence it was thought at the outset of mission work that, for the conversion of the Mohammedans, an attempt must be made to reform the Oriental Churches. Could the golden candlesticks be relighted, and Armenian and Greek worshippers become true witnesses for Jesus, the reflection of gospel truth would shine over vast spaces of Asia, and an effective agency might be extensively utilized. But there has not been any great quickening of Oriental Christianity, and the later policy has been that of independent organization.

It is no longer a capital offence, as it was a few years ago, for a Moslem to change his religion. Recently, at Beirut, a prominent follower of the Prophet became a disciple of Jesus. Appeal was made to civil authority, and an injunction obtained. Arraigned before a legal tribunal, and threatened with the consequences of turning renegade, he was permitted to bear a striking testimony to the truth. Taking a copy of the New Testament from beneath his robe, amid the breathless silence of the court the convert read the first chapter of St. John's Gospel; and with intense earnestness he spoke of the true Light, of the Word made flesh, and of the Lamb of God that taketh away the sin of the world. But, while a certain amount of tolerance has been granted by law, drawbacks and disabilities of conversion are such as to prevent any except the most decided inquirers from making a public renunciation of Islam, or a profession of the Christian faith.

There are signs, however, of a waning Crescent. The march of Moslem armies has been described as a thunderbolt of war; but the cloud that bears the burning bolt must move on or be dissolved. Political unity, the result of conquest, has long formed the citadel of Mohammedan strength. Religion and politics are fused. Threatened disintegration of Turkish power must therefore be regarded as a hopeful feature in the problem of access to Moslem populations. Should Mohammedans cease to be a political power, buttressed by great European empires, the Koran may come fairly into competition with the Bible, and detected impostures of the false Prophet lead to an examination and acceptance of the claims of the Lord Jesus Christ. The unity of the Godhead appeals to Islam sentiment, forms an initial base of accordance, and may lead to common ground in regard to other fundamental truths. Only let pure Christianity and the Arabian imposture be brought into candid comparison, and prejudice must melt away. The Moslem worshipper of the One God shall be led to believe in Jesus Christ the Son of God, the Saviour of the world.

The Crescent must surely fall before the Cross. A venerable mosque at Damascus, once a Christian church, and in pagan times a heathen temple, perpetuates a record of prophetic hope and anticipation. An inscription on its portal, carved in Greek character, proclaims the permanence of the Saviour's spiritual empire. Centuries of Mohammedan fanaticism and deep hatred to Christianity seemed to contradict the silent prediction. No follower of the Nazarene was permitted, during a long dark period, to tread the courts of that sanctuary. But when missionaries of the Presbyterian Church entered upon their enterprise in that ancient city of Syria, they deciphered the inscription, and had faith to believe it true: "Thy kingdom, O Christ, is an everlasting kingdom, and Thy dominion endureth throughout all generations."

There is said to be a Moslem belief that the latter days shall witness a universal apostacy from the Islam faith, and that the Koran shall cease to exist. Are not the evangelical Churches summoned at once to the occupancy of new fields, and to the achievement of greater spiritual conquest? Obstacles are all but innumerable. The work is great. Missions to Mohammedans ought to possess a distinctive character. Responsibility is not to be left to a section of the sacramental host. No single denomination should bear the brunt of assault on the faith of Islam. *Let the whole line advance!*

Christianity has vested rights in Mohammedan lands, many a claim which she cannot forego. An old traveller, Von Schubert, musing at the mosque of St. Sophia, experienced an emotion of sadness. The thought of a long desecration produced a feeling somewhat resembling that of a Northman, whose son, at Algiers, was found wearing the garb and leading the life of a Turkish renegade. The followers of Jesus had not dared since its surrender to enter that once renowned sanctuary of the Christian faith—through which the magnificent *Te Deum* had been wont to resound,—and only when passing had ventured to glance into its courts. How long must the minstrel wait outside the prison walls, like *Cœur de Leon*, till they from within should strike up the well-known hymns of praise and thanksgiving? "The minstrel of thy Saviour tarries long. And thou, old belfry, thou art but small beside the minarets and golden crescents; but when thy voice returns to thee, it shall sound over sea and land like the call of the muezzin."

There is a strong temptation, as we near the Ægean

or the Bosphorus, following in the track of the first great missionary, crossing the Straits from Asia into Europe, to pursue a still westward course. Philippopolis and Salonika, where St. Paul preached the gospel, are occupied as mission stations. But the unspeakable Turk still rules, and the Christian hears the voice as of old: "Come over into Macedonia and help us."

A Mediterranean voyage takes us to the African continent. The Barbary States, extending from Morocco to Egypt, are said to comprise over fifteen million people, of whom four hundred thousand are reported "Christians" of some sort, three hundred thousand Jews, and the rest Mohammedans. Except in the case of missions to the Jews in Algiers and Tunis, very little is being done to lead those erring ones into the way of life. Once along the northern border line of the African continent, as we have seen, there were flourishing Christian Churches. But that "green strip" was long ago desolated by the sands of Moslem invasion. Was the cause of failure to be found in the fact, as some believe, that the early Churches were satisfied to be lights only along the shore, and that no attempt was made to carry the lamp of salvation to the benighted ones of the interior? Missionary churches do not die. Only through unfaithfulness to her responsibilities could African Christianity be conquered by fierce invaders.

For purposes of spiritual conquest Egypt must be

regarded as one of the strategic points of Africa. It is the stronghold of Arabian slavery. The river Nile forms a connection with the interior of the continent. Here, too, may be found the *Tel el Kebir* of Mohammedanism. The great university of Cairo, with its three hundred attaches, enrols an attendance of ten thousand students; and from El Azrah, as emissaries of the Islam faith, educated bands find their way to the centre of Africa, to the eastern part of Asia, and to the Isles of the Sea. With the exception of six hundred thousand Copts, the five and a half million of people in Egypt proper, and the nearly eleven and a half million of annexed territory, are Mohammedans. The United Presbyterian Church prosecutes an influential Copt mission on the Nile, and the Church of England is reorganizing a mission to the Moslem population. The victorious banner of a British host should be succeeded by the sacred standard of the Cross. Wonders shall God work again in the land of Zoan. "The Lord shall be known in Egypt, and Egypt shall know the Lord."

Ethiopia, in which the London Society has a mission, has frequent association with Egypt in the language of prophecy. An Abyssinian Church claims a Christian name and character. But the light that once was in her has become darkness. No part of the world has more need of the gospel than the regions of the Upper Nile.

Zanquebar and Mozambique, along the eastern coast

of Africa, have yet to be occupied by the advanced posts of Christianity. But the little island of Zanzibar, adjoining the continent, forming a convenient base for interior enterprise, is held as the headquarters of the Universities' Mission. The old slave market, where in recent years there was an annual sale of thirty thousand slaves, has been turned into a scene of beneficent influence, forming the site of a church, mission-house, and schools. Thirty-four European missionaries, and a number of native evangelists, constitute an effective corps for the prosecution of aggressive enterprise. From the sea coast a line of stations has been carried towards the central lakes. The grave of Bishop Mackenzie, a missionary hero, is three hundred miles inland. But that way-mark is only on the threshold of new and accessible territory. "Beyond and beyond," said his successor, Bishop Steere, another brave leader whose brief course has been finished, "lie nations after nations, until the mind is overwhelmed by the vastness of the work before us."

To Madagascar, the magnificent island on the east of the Mozambique Channel, must be awarded the crown of modern missions. Facts in regard to the rapid abandonment of idolatry, especially in the central provinces, are well known. Equally extraordinary have been the accessions of converts to the Christian ranks. The London Society reports an aggregate of twelve hundred churches, five thousand native preachers, eighty thousand communicants, and not less than half a million of adherents. A million of dollars has been contributed, during a single decade, for the spread of the gospel. Malagasy Christians realize a sense of responsibility in regard to the promotion of the Saviour's work; and, at the Mildmay Conference, the belief was expressed by a Madagascar missionary that these churches would rise to the level of yet greater things, and take their share in the hope and hazard of winning the continent for Christ.

From the eastern coast, missionaries have penetrated to the interior of Africa; and, in a marvellous manner, central regions and races have become accessible to Christianity. The Church of England has reinforced her oft-shattered and depleted ranks, and extended her mission posts to Victoria Nyanza. A promising Blantyre Mission of the Church of Scotland has been planted on the healthful heights of the Shire region. In memory of Africa's best friend, a noble and fitting monument, the Free Church of Scotland has started successfully her Livingstonia enterprise. Eight years after its discovery, in October 1875, the sparkling waters of the Nyassa burst upon the view of the Scotch pioneer missionaries. The Hundreth Psalm,

> "All people that on earth do dwell
> Sing to the Lord with cheerful voice,"

seemed to have a new beauty and depth of meaning as its notes floated over the blue waves of the spacious lake. Two steamers, the *Lady Nyassa* on the Zambesi and Shire rivers and the *Itala* on Lake Nyassa, form an easy route from the coast. Beyond the northern shore of the Nyassa, deeper into the interior, an explorer pushes on to the Tanganyika; a great inland sea, on the eastern and western shores of which, amidst a dense population, the London Society is planting its vigorous missions. Does not the day dawn for Africa? From the east and the west pioneer forces are pressing to the heart of the continent. The watchword has been sounded: *"Forward to the centre!"*

South Africa was early a storied land of missions. The Moravian brethren sent their first missionary to the Hottentots in 1737, and they have now thirty-nine laborers in the field; while one of their stations, Mamre, has a roll of one thousand and three hundred communicants. The London Society, with headquarters at Kuruman in Bechuanaland, has twenty-two missionaries, a strong staff of native helpers, and a large membership. United Presbyterian and Free Churches of Scotland carry on an influential work in Kaffraria. Wesleyan missionaries, entering the field at an early period, starting from the Cape, have extended colonial and native stations to little Namaqualand on the one hand, and to the Zulu country on the other. One hundred stations of the Church of England Propagation Society comprise colonial and native missions. The American Board has an encouraging Zulu cause. Dutch and other missionaries labor in the Transvaal. Several Continental societies have agents in South African territory.

Western Africa, following the coast line from the south, completes the circuit of mission stations. Missionaries of the American Board have inaugurated a new enterprise at Benguela. English Baptists are steaming up the Congo to a thickly-populated central region, and the Livingstone Inland Mission forwards evangelists by the same route. What an immense field opens up for the diffusion of the gospel in the vast Congo valley! It is computed that in order to furnish a single missionary to the thickly-peopled towns and villages, scattered over each hundred square miles, no less than nine thousand men would be needed. The reflection of missionary watch-fires can be seen over a dark region at the mouth of the Niger. Wesleyan and Church of England societies maintain their stations along the line of the Gold Coast and at Sierra Leone. More than one hundred and twenty messengers of the gospel, during a period of forty years, have succumbed to the effects of deadly climate,

> "And their low pillow has been the strange soil
> Of that distant and grave-dotted strand."

But the work has not been in vain in the Lord. Communicants of the several stations now number thirty thousand.

As from the shores of Africa we embark for this Western continent—such is the magnitude of the work yet to be accomplished—the Macedonian cry, heard from many lands, still sounds along our course, and mingles with the murmur of the mighty main. Souls benighted plead for light and help.

> "Christians, hearken: none has taught them
> Of the Saviour's love so dear;
> Of the precious price that bought them;
> Of the nail, the thorn, the spear.
> Ye who know Him,
> Guide them from the darkness drear."

When shall " the wail of the billows of humanity," from the lands of idolatry, from scenes of Moslem superstition, from Asia and Africa, and from the Isles of the sunny South, be turned into a shout of rejoicing?

"There is yet no more than time to open an enterprise so vast. But already there are materials from which it is possible to estimate the prospects of the missionary enterprise, and the grandeur of the results which its success must yield."—*Robert Mackenzie.*

VI.

PROGRESS AND RESULTS OF FOREIGN MISSIONS.

THE missions of this century, as far as can be ascertained from available and reliable data, began with a membership of not more than fifty thousand. But now missionary communicants are estimated at over half a million, and nearly three and a half million of adherents have been won from heathenism. Such an exhibit is full of encouragement. Ratio constantly increases. Reduplication is marvellous. The accessions of a single year are larger than was the aggregate of converts at the commencement of the century.

A brief statistical summary is all that can be attempted on this page. Central and South America, including the West Indies, with a population of over thirty-five million, where four hundred and thirty commissioned messengers of the cross are seeking to respond to the Macedonian cry, began the present decade with a return of twenty-five thousand communicants, forty-three thousand scholars, and eighty thousand attendants on public worship. Asia, an immense territory, stretching from the Sea of Sinim to the Hellespont, and from the sands of Arabia to the snows of Siberia, with a population of eight hundred million, in which two thousand five hundred missionaries are sounding forth the word of life, seeking to turn men "from idols to serve the living and true God," is credited with nearly two hundred and forty-six thousand communicants, two hundred and eighteen thousand scholars, and three hundred and forty-three thousand adherents. Oceanica missions, comprising several groups of islands, where a brave band of consecrated men, inclusive of a proportionately large native element, are seeking to win bright trophies for Jesus, aggregates one hundred and twenty thousand communicants, seventy-five thousand scholars, and five hundred and thirty thousand nominal Christians. Africa, with two hundred million of people, where, including Madagascar and Mauritius, nine hundred missionaries proclaim the gospel of peace and goodwill, presents a roll of nearly one hundred and sixty-five thousand communicants, over ninety-eight thousand scholars, and five hundred and eighteen thousand worshippers reclaimed from the baseness and barbarities of heathenism. European missions, comprising stations in Spain, France, Italy, Greece, Turkey, Bulgaria, and some other places that sorely need a second Reformation, where seven hundred evangelists are seeking to propagate a purer faith, return ninety-six thousand communicants. But even these summaries are far from being exhaustive of the whole field of missions.*

---

* "Probably," says Dr. Dorchester, in his valuable and suggestive statistical exhibit of missions for 1880, "more than 20,000 stations are occupied. More than 40,000 laborers, lay and clerical, are in

missionary progress, and many great and glorious spiritual results, do not admit of tabular exhibit.

Several years ago a writer in the *Times* complained that the reports of the several foreign missionary societies were not made up in a satisfactory manner. There was said to be an "absence of those facts, those details, that account of results," which generous contributors "require in every matter they take in hand." But no longer can there be any cause for dissatisfaction on that ground. Statistics are abundantly tabulated. Leading principles and details are so grasped and grouped as to become mutually illustrative and explanatory; and, in marked contrast, with most impressive effect, they are projected against the dark and discouraging background of a preceding era.

The most exhaustive summaries, however, in this period of expansion, must soon be out of date, and can only be valuable as way-marks of progress. The vast impetus of advancing evangelical movement necessitates constant revision of numerical statement. But there are some special results of modern missions that can never lose their significance, and to which the

---

the foreign fields, 131 missions not reporting the former and 51 not reporting the latter item—probably 45,000 at least of these laborers. From 356 of the 504 missions we have 857,332 communicants reported. Returns from the remaining 148 would doubtless swell the aggregate to over 1,000,000. These figures do not include nominal converts from heathenism, but enrolled Church members. The nominal adherents or hearers, reported in about two-fifths of the missions, are 1,813,596—probably about three and a half millions in all."— *Problem of Religious Progress*, pp. 487, 488.

publication of annual and decennial returns only challenges renewed attention :—

The area of enterprise has been immensely enlarged.
There was a contraction of Christian work, in even the comparatively recent past, which is not easy for us to understand. A most chilling subject, at any time between the decline of the Puritan and the rise of the Wesleyan movement, was that of the world's evangelization. Two centuries ago a number of gifted and godly ministers were silenced in England, excluded from the pulpits of the Established Church. Saintly Richard Baxter grieved greatly for the loss of such a ministry. But the chief sorrow was in the fact that these men could not be utilized as missionaries to the heathen. He was led in this way to ponder the question of obligation in relation to the great commission. England had been wont to absorb his thoughts; or if the rest of the world was considered, a prayer for the conversion of the Jews was almost all. But when he came to understand the condition of the heathen nations, their need of the gospel, and "the method of the Lord's Prayer," there was nothing so heavy upon his heart as the thought of the miseries of unenlightened lands of the earth. Even the calamities of his friends or of his country could not affect him so much as the case of heathen, Mohammedan, and ignorant people of dark and distant regions. 'Could we but go among Tartars, Turks, and heathen, I should be but little troubled for the silencing of eighteen hundred ministers at once in England;

which maketh me greatly honor Mr. John Eliot, the apostle of the Indians in New England." It is difficult to realize that, as late as the seventeenth century, with the exception of a little strip along the eastern seaboard, this continent of America, the whole of Africa, the teeming millions of China and India, the greatest part of Asia, the lands of the Bible, and the numerous Isles of the Sea, were utterly inaccessible to the missionary of the cross or any evangelistic agency.

Even at the commencement of this mission century the doors of heathendom were almost everywhere closed. It is well known that when William Carey set his face towards the East no English ship would tolerate a missionary passenger, and he had to sail under the Danish flag. "If I ever see a Hindoo converted to Jesus Christ," said Henry Martyn, in his day, "I shall see something more nearly approaching the resurrection of a dead body than anything I have ever yet seen." Dr. Morrison landed at Macao in 1807. The attempt to make Christians out of Chinese Buddhists was generally regarded as a Utopian and utterly hopeless scheme. It was stigmatized as an "absurdity in hysterics, preposterousness run mad, illusion dancing in the maddening frenzy, the unsubstantial dream and vision of a dreamer who dreams that he has been dreaming." The West India slave continued to clank the chain of a bitter and relentless bondage. Dwellers in the Southern Archipelago were still enveloped in the impenetrable gloom of heathen night. Deeper than Egyptian darkness brooded over the continent of Africa. It was claimed to be yet an open question as to the capability of sable races for elevation in the scale of civilization; and, in reference to the negro, James Montgomery met the doubt by a pathetic plea:

> "Since his wrongs began,
> His follies and his crimes have stampt him Man."

It was affirmed by politicians and officials of the East India Company that were an attempt made to interfere with the religion of Hindustan, insult would be quickly resented, the people of India would sweep away the Anglo-Saxon race and rule, with as much ease as the sand of the desert is driven by an east wind; and down to the mutiny, 1857, as tidings of disaster reached the India House, a director exultingly exclaimed, "Now we shall get rid of the saints!" The thick wall of Chinese exclusiveness had been scarcely pierced. Oriental tongues were but little understood, and but few uncivilized languages had been reduced to writing.

Marvellous has been the change! Barriers of ages have been broken down. Antipathies are relaxed or repressed. The world is everywhere accessible. South Seas have been flooded with light. Africa is being explored and claimed for Christ. From Cape Comorin to the distant Himalayas, India is becoming a vast and fruitful mission field. China, to her western mountains, and her northern wall, welcomes the heralds of salvation. In lands where, within the memory of living missionaries, through the prevalence of repulsive and sanguinary rites and superstitions, the people were oppressed, the earth polluted, and heaven insulted, Christian congregations now gather for prayer and praise. There is also a prodigious growth of intercommunication. Steam speeds the missionary to his distant post, and electricity flashes back the tidings of progress. "To me," says the venerable Bishop Simpson, "all this portends the coming of an era of universal light and glory."

Missions have added stirring and storied pages to the history of spiritual achievement.

What literature of this world, in thrilling and romantic interest, can surpass that of modern missions? It was once said that the narrative of John Williams' mission to the South Sea Islands might be regarded as the twenty-ninth chapter in the Acts of the Apostles. A writer in a current number of "The Gospel in all Lands" says, "The achievements of the missionary enterprises of to-day are only the Book of Acts continued on into the nineteenth century." The tours of St. Paul and his companions, their intrepidity and successes, form a fascinating part of the inspired history. But the writer of that narrative could not chronicle all the *acts* of the Christian Church. There is no sign or seal of completeness, no finish or formula, at the close of the book. The record runs on from Antioch to Galatia, and from the mission scenes of Asia to the populous cities of Europe. Not for a moment, to the very last verse, is there any abatement of missionary spirit and interest: "preaching the kingdom of God, and teaching the things which concern the Lord Jesus Christ." The history of magnificent enterprise, and of the spread of early Christianity, thus closes with an apparent abruptness. As you stroll amongst partially hewn blocks, scattered about the quarries of the Nile, retaining in that salubrious clime their freshness for long centuries, you almost look for the workman to return with mallet and chisel, and to complete the partially wrought column or slab. Some such feeling one may have after an eager perusal of the Acts of the Apostles. We wait for more. The cross has been victorious in voluptuous Antioch, gorgeous Corinth, idolatrous Ephesus, and in imperial Rome. But what of the spread of the gospel through the provinces of Gaul and Spain? Were not the victories of imperial legions surpassed by those of the armies of the cross? By what agency were fierce and uncivilized hordes of "those northern and inclement Scandinavian shores, which made the lordly Roman shiver when he named them," subjugated to the faith of Christ? We almost expect the inspired writer to resume his pen, to chronicle new facts of apostolic achievement, and to complete the marvellous narrative.

Is it not evidently the Divine idea that the sacred record, acts of men who hazarded their lives for the Lord Jesus, should be supplemented by reports of evangelistic enterprise, and of soul-saving work, until the great consummation shall have been won?

The history of spiritual achievement repeats itself. Acts of the Apostles furnish an admirable model for the reports of modern missions. Missionary movements in the nineteenth century are simply a reproduction of early Christianity. The first messengers of the cross, as they left Antioch for the foreign work, were "recommended to the grace of God," and followed by the prayers of all the disciples. In like manner, a consecrated band of men and women, recently leaving American shores for China and the eastern parts of Asia, were fervently commended to Divine care and protection, and accompanied by the prayers and hopes of many Christian people of the United States. The incident of Barnabas and Paul sailing away to Cyprus, and across the Pamphylian Gulf, always retains its freshness and power. Later pages glow with the grand enthusiasm of such missionaries as Carey and Coke, rocking on the mighty ocean, and planning the conquest of new continents for Christ. Opening chapters of the Book of Acts in the New Testament tell of the martyrdom of St. Stephen and of St. James, beaten with stones or slain with the sword. Modern annals immortalize the martyrs of Erromanga and Madagascar, and the names of the heroic men who are falling at their post in Central Africa. An indescribable charm is associated with the first days of the gospel in Corinth and in Philippi ; but the facts of Serampore and Kuruman, and a hundred other places, furnish evidence of a gloriously perpetuated apostolic succession. Through the zeal of mission Churches planted by St. Paul and his fellow-laborers, the word of the Lord was sounded out, "not only in Macedonia and Achaia, but also in every place." A spirit of propagandism is being developed in the native Churches of India and South Africa, of Hawaii and Tonga, that gives a noble impulse to the onward movement of modern Christianity. Yes, there is abundant material for supplementary chapters to "the Acts of the Apostles."

It is sometimes complained that the statistical portions of missionary reports are not attractive. Would any one complain that a page of a Parliamentary Bluebook was duller than the latest work of fiction, or that bulletins of battle were wanting in imaginative and literary power and expression? To the political economist, statistical exhibits furnish information in the most compact and available form; and, to hearts strained by palpitating and protracted anxiety and suspense, eager for the details of national conflict, rhetorical flourish would seem sadly out of place. Reports of mission work are put into business form, so far as statistics and summaries are concerned. But, between the lines, thoughtful men and women find a world of meaning. Beneath the tabulated statements, there are exhibitions of patience and intrepidity of spirit, of unselfish and successful work for Christ, that move the soul alternately to exultation and to tears.

Apart from purely business reports, the Church has a great missionary literature, which, for magnificence of range, variety, romance of fact and incident, touching and thrilling detail and power, surpasses all other publications of the age.* Dr. Jabez Bunting once said that he read the leading newspapers of the day in order to understand the manner in which his heavenly Father governed the world. Those who would keep abreast of the marvellous changes that are being wrought in the earth, and who would mark the victories that signalize the march of spiritual empire, must ransack the records of evangelical enterprise, and saturate their minds with the memorials of missionary heroes.

Modern Missions have greatly enriched the biographies of the Christian Church.

The Epistle to the Hebrews has a chapter of unrivalled interest, which has been characterized as "the Westminster Abbey of the New Testament." The names of heroes of the Hebrew faith are there embalmed. Where shall we now find a succession to that inspired bead-roll of immortal fame? To what sphere must we look for the noblest manifestations of human life and heroism? The men and women who, far away from scenes of show and ostentation, have consecrated themselves to the missionary cause,

---

* Two new book-lists happen to be at hand, as these lines are written, and they announce or notice such volumes as those of Dr. Christlieb's "Foreign Missions," the magnificent "Ely Volume" of Dr. Laurie, Bambridge's "Around the World of Christian Missions," Thompson's "Moravian Missions," "The Sunrise Kingdom," "Life in Greece and Palestine," and a "History of Indian Missions on the Pacific Coast."

to spend and to be spent for Christ, constitute a goodly fellowship. In spiritual resolve and intrepid deed, the line of missionary succession streams and blazes with holy and heavenly light. Names of peerless renown, Xavier and Schwartz, Eliot and Egede, Carey and Coke, Morrison and Mills, Judson and Marshman, Henry Martyn and Reginald Heber, Robert Moffat and William Shaw, John Williams and John Hunt, Alexander Duff and David Livingstone, Coleridge Patteson and Charles Frederic Mackenzie, John Geddie and Charles New, James Evans and George McDougal, must *forever* shine in a galaxy of splendor. "Read only the life of Patteson," says Max Muller, "the Bishop of Melanesia. It has been my privilege to have known some of the finest and noblest spirits which England has produced during this century, but there is none to whose memory I look up with greater reverence, none by whose friendship I feel more deeply humbled, than that of that true saint, true martyr, and truly parental missionary." *

The dust of another honored missionary has been rendered to the mould in trophied tomb and temple. A magnificent sepulchre was prepared for the mortal remains of the great pioneer of African missions. It was a fitting recognition which the world freely accorded to daring and intrepidity, unswerving goodness and patient achievement.

---

* *On Missions*, Ecl. Review, 1874, p. 263.

> "We saw them lower him to rest:
> Was ever human bosom pressed
> By dust more manly? Or a name
> Of humble origin and fame
> Linked firmer to the heart of man?
> Or life's most transient human span
> Crowded with grander, nobler deeds?"

But is there need to chant the requiem, weave the chaplet, or carve the monument of stone? Do not deeds of missionary devotion find a higher than earthly record and recompense? "And they that be wise shall shine as the brightness of the firmament; and they that turn many to righteousness as the stars for ever and ever."

The names of a devoted sisterhood have been immortalized by the inspired Apostle Paul: Phebe, "a succourer of many and of myself also;" Priscilla, "a helper in Christ Jesus;" Mary, "who bestowed much labor on us;" Tryphena and Tryphosa, "who labor in the Lord;" the beloved Persis, "which laboreth much in the Lord." But what New Testament record, "of honorable women not a few," can surpass that of modern missions? Harriet Newell and Mary Cryer, the wives of Judson, Mary Moffat and Mary M. Ellis, Fidelia Fiske and Harriet C. Mullens, Dorothy Jones and Rebecca Wakefield, and others whose lives have been equally consecrated, heroines of the missionary enterprise, may claim an enduring inscription. In each case, the Saviour's approval is sure: "She hath done what she could." "Verily I say unto you, wheresoever this gospel shall be preached throughout the whole world, this also that she hath done shall be spoken for a memorial of her."

Missionaries have made numerous translations of the Bible into varied languages of the earth.

One of the most wonderful facts of modern missions, completely changing the aspect and atmosphere of the Christian world, is the immense impetus given to the work of disseminating the sacred Scriptures. It is not always easy to understand the stupendous toil demanded for the work of translation. Equivalents for words freighted with evangelical significance, such as sin, atonement, and righteousness, are exceedingly difficult to obtain. The Burmese version of Dr. Judson, regarded as a noble work, cost him nineteen years of hard toil. Dr. Carey devoted fifteen years of unremitting labor to his Bengali version. The Arabic translation was a work of fifteen, and that of Tahiti twenty years. Mainly through the unwearied effort of scholarly missionaries, during the past eighty years, the Word of God—or portions of the Old and New Testament—has been rendered into numerous living languages. Had there been no other mission results, this great achievement would alone have constituted an ample compensation for the expenditure of life and treasure. Some one has said that the most profound homage which may be offered to a creature, reserved from genius and earthly grandeur, from the soldier that wins blood-stained wreaths, from the statesman that controls courts and cabinets, and from the orator whose thoughts and words breathe and burn, shall be gratefully paid to him who first makes a wide-spoken tongue to utter words of salvation.

There were thought to be at the commencement of this century, existing in fifty languages, about five million copies of the Scriptures. But in 1882, a single year, the issues of the Bible Society, and of three kindred institutions, aggregated nearly five million of copies. The Word of God has been rendered into no less than three hundred languages and dialects, comprising the speech of nine-tenths of the population of the globe. Is not the Bible the modern gift of tongues?

As in the mystic river of sanctuary vision, the life-giving streams of sacred truth are progressive and efficacious. The waters deepened in their flow, to the ankles, to the knees, and up to the loins, not too deep for a man to wade through, from brink to brink. But, suddenly, and without apparent cause, the river became a mighty flood; "for the waters were risen, waters to swim in, a river that could not be passed over." There was also a marvellous efficacy in those holy waters. "And everything shall live whither the river cometh." Through waste and wild, deep gorge and gloomy ravine, a wealth of tropical vegetation beautifies and enriches its course. The Dead Sea, a region of sand, salt, and sulphur, is penetrated and purified. Sluggish depths are healed. "And by the river, upon the banks thereof, on this side and on that side, shall grow all trees for meat, whose leaf shall not fade, neither shall the fruit thereof be consumed: it shall bring forth new fruit according to his months, because their waters they issued out of the sanctuary; and the fruit thereof shall be meat, and the leaf thereof for medicine."

Missions have demonstrated the essential manhood of degraded races.

It has been found that man everywhere has a capacity for the reception of spiritual truth. Carey spoke of going "down into the mine" of degraded humanity, and he and his fellow-laborers penetrated to some of its darkest and foulest depths. Once it was affirmed that nothing precious could be found at such a level of baseness and depression. But missionary explorers have been richly rewarded. They have struck rich veins, and have brought to the surface treasures of splendid worth. The possibilities of redeemed races have been proved. Through the power and process of saving and sanctifying truth and grace, gems of immortal mind, freed from foul encrustation, polished and beautified, flash with the light of Christian graces and of an expanded intellect.

By what standard shall we attempt to measure the importance of such a work? The Apostle Paul had a profound impression of the worth of redeemed humanity. Once he was instrumental in the salvation of a runaway slave, Onesimus, and the elation of feeling produced by that success prompted him to write the Epistle of Philemon. The conversion of one heathen soul—a dusky child of the forest, a dark dweller of ice-bound Labrador, a Hindu devotee, a savage Kaffir, a degraded Malagasian, a barbarous Tongan, a senseless Papuan, or a stupid Patagonian—is worth more than the outlay demanded by the costliest missions. The lowest of all these tribes may not only be raised to a higher grade of civilization, but to the dignity of sons and heirs of God. An eminent scientist, Charles R. Darwin, while cruising off the coast of South America, making the observations which formed the foundation of his lifework as a naturalist, noticed the degraded condition of the Patagonians. He was positive in discussion of the subject that they were specifically different from the races of Europe, and absolutely incapable of improvement. In later years, as he came to understand the success of the Church of England missionaries in promoting a Patagonian civilization, "he frankly avowed his mistake, and gave his name as a subscriber to the funds of the South American Society—on whose books it still, remains."*

Missions furnish evidence of the adaptation of the Gospel of Christ to all conditions of human need.

The gospel of Jesus Christ has been given to dark idolaters of Oriental lands and to the forest wanderers of this western continent, to the polar seal-hunter and to the negro slave; and everywhere, amid Arctic snows

---

*The fact is vouched for by a correspondent of the *Manchester Guardian.*

and at the burning tropics, it has been found efficacious, "the power of God unto salvation to every one that believeth." As light to the eye, or melody to the ear, exquisite in its adaptation, the gospel of Christ finds its way to the human soul, and satisfies the heart as nothing else can do. There was a time when Moravian missionaries thought that the Esquimaux were too dark and degraded to receive the sublime teachings of Christianity. They must first aim at an improved civilization. Moral precepts, and the first principles of natural religion were earnestly inculcated. But the experiment of years proved to be an utter failure. No progress was made on that line of effort. It was like ploughing and sowing on rocks or fields of ice. But patiently they toiled in the laborious work of preparing a version of the Gospels for Greenland. One memorable day, natives lingered round John Beck and questioned him about the writing. The Missionary read a few sentences, and for the first time in that land announced the "faithful saying, and worthy of all acceptation, that Christ Jesus came into the world to save sinners." As he spoke of the sufferings of Christ, his own soul was filled with emotion. Then he read to the wondering listeners, in their own language, the account of the Redeemer's agony in Gethsemane. "How was that," asked one of the men, a wild savage from the mountains, "tell us that again, for we too would be saved?" Again, with softened heart and streaming eyes, they listened to the wondrous story of Jesus and His love; and, after their wonted manner, when struck dumb with amazement, they put their hands upon their mouths. One anxious inquirer was savingly converted to God. This first convert, Kajarnak, became a teacher to his countrymen, and to the end of his life adorned his profession. The Moravian pioneers obtained a clearer idea of the Divine method of saving men, savage and civilized, and from that time resolved to preach nothing "save Jesus Christ and Him crucified."

In the mission of the brave and brotherly George McDougal, there was an incident illustrative of the power of the gospel and its adaptation to all classes and conditions of men. The Missionary has gathered a considerable congregation of Indians, many of whom have been brought under the influence of Christianity and civilization. But yonder on the outskirts of the prairie audience is a fierce pagan chief who scorns to accept a new religion, or to depart from the traditions of his tribe. Paint and feathers, tomahawk or rifle, still bespeak the savage. But the preacher believes that his quiver contains a sharp arrow that may cleave its way to the heart and conscience of that rude barbarian. A telling sentence rouses his indignant interest. "And what is it," he demands, dismounting from his horse, and stalking proudly up to the front of the missionary, "that you have to tell me that will make my heart glad?" The preacher understands the Indian character and passionateness of purpose, but he has faith in his message, and believes it to be "good tidings of great joy, which shall be to all people." There are chords in that dusky warrior's soul, which, if skilfully touched, must respond to the truth; and, in earnest and tender tones and true, he tells of "Jesus and the resurrection." Hardness and scorn are conquered; and the haughty chief, who perhaps had never shed a tear, except at the grave of a darling child, astounded by the words that the dead shall rise again, softens to sensibility and contrite feeling.

"Never," says a lady-worker in the Eastern mission field, "has the old, old story seemed so sweet as when it was told to those dark-eyed and darker-minded women to whom *it was not old.* The lighting up of dull faces, when first their hearts take in the wonderful fact of a Saviour's love to them, and their eager questionings in regard to the good news, lead to a realization of the blessedness of the work."

But why should isolated instances of Divine and saving power be selected and adduced? Every mission in every land exhibits the efficacy of the gospel. When John the Baptist was in prison—a moment of depression it might have been—he sent messengers to the Saviour to know if he were indeed the Christ that should come. "Jesus answered and said unto them, Go and shew John again those things which ye do hear and see: The blind receive their sight, and the lame walk, the lepers are cleansed, and the deaf hear, the dead are raised up, and the poor have the gospel preached to them." Need we other attestation of the power of the gospel. Darkness is dispelled.

Sinners are converted. Monuments of mercy are being daily multiplied.

> "Jesus the prisoner's fetters breaks,
> And bruises Satan's head ;
> Power into strengthless souls it speaks,
> And life into the dead."

Missions make important contributions to commerce, literature, and science.

No one can doubt the value of missionary contribution to the cause of civilization and the world's progress. Even, if there were only financial tests to be met, and evangelical enterprise had no sublimer aspects, the gain has been immense. Most of the trade of Lagos, amounting to four million dollars a year, according to the testimony of Sir T. Fowell Buxton, is due to the industry of the christianized natives of Sierra Leone. A century ago, Captain Cook was murdered on the Sandwich Islands, and missionaries found a degraded and savage people, living in the surf and on the sand, devouring raw flesh, and steeped in sensuality. But now Honolulu, the Hawaiin capital, is an important commercial port, with a flourishing and legitimate traffic of three million of dollars annually. It has been calculated that every missionary in the South Seas creates on an average a trade of fifty thousand dollars a year. Leading merchants of London and Glasgow, believing that commercially their investment will be a good one, and that a great impulse will be given to the development of trade, have contributed to Central

African missions. Footprints of missionary pioneers are a safe and sure track for the trader. A member of the British Parliament, one of the merchant princes of the sea-girt isle, standing up lately in the busy city of Manchester, brought home the question to the practical sense of business men. He claimed that in the great metropolis of manufacturing interests, from which productions of the loom were going out to civilized and uncivilized parts of the world, there was nothing undignified in the introduction or consideration of the subject of Christian missions. Commercial men might be appealed to even on subordinate grounds to support this spiritual enterprise. The missionary was the pioneer of mercantile interests. Many a valuable market, for years and years to come, would have been closed to their Lancashire manufactures had it not been that heroic missionaries had first led the way in an attempt to raise heathen people in the scale of civilization. They were bound to support the missionary societies very much more nobly than they had done in the past. "I think," said Mr. Mason, "that the obligation rests upon them as commercial men, even as much as it rests upon them as Christian men, to be more liberal in their contributions."

The missionary, as he penetrates the stupidity and barbarities of paganism, is followed by the plough, the loom, the printing-press, the lighthouse, the telegraph and the railway. Every new mission to lands of uncivilized heathenism, originated and sustained by the Christian Church, expands the wings of commerce,

RESULTS OF FOREIGN MISSIONS. 181

slips another belt on the complicated machinery of modern civilization, and makes its influence felt in the markets of the globe.

Science and literature have also been greatly promoted. The study of numerous languages develops linguistic and philological genius and aptness, and hence the special value of missionary contributions. "Nothing," it is said in regard to Livingstone, "can be more telling than his life as an evidence of the power and truth of Christianity, as a plea for Christian missions and civilization, or as a demonstration of the true connection between religion and science." * The *Missionary Herald* is placed by an eminent German geographer, Karl Ritter, above all scientific magazines as a repository of "scientific, historical, and antiquarian details." The recently-published Ely volume, devoted to "missions and science," furnishes a magnificent summary of material results. "Mission agents," says the *Times* in a recent editorial, "penetrate where officials and private persons have no wish and no call to penetrate, and they enable us to realize wants and needs of whose existence we should often otherwise be dimly conscious."

The valuable influence of missionaries, in the promotion of national interests and the general good of heathen communities, has been repeatedly acknowledged. It was the opinion of the late Lord Lawrence, Governor-General of India, and one of the greatest

---

* Dr. Blaikie's *Life of David Livingstone*, Preface.

and best men that England ever gave to her Eastern empire, notwithstanding all that the Government had done for that country, that "missionaries have done more than all agencies combined." "I speak simply as to matters of experience and observation," said Sir Bartle Frere, in 1874, "just as a Roman Prefect might have reported to Trajan or the Antonines; and I assure you that the teaching of Christianity among a hundred and sixty millions of civilized and industrious Hindus and Mohammedans in India is effecting changes—moral, social, and political—which for extent and rapidity of effect are far more extraordinary than anything you or your fathers have witnessed in modern Europe." The Government of India, according to an official document printed by order of the House of Commons, acknowledges "the great obligation under which it is laid by the benevolent exertions of these six hundred missionaries, whose blameless example and self-denying labors are infusing new vigor into the stereotyped life of the great populations placed under English rule, and preparing them to be in every way better men and better citizens."*

Facts of missionary progress and achievement, extended area of enterprise, glowing narratives of pioneer toil and triumph, exhibitions of heroism and saintly devotion, translations of the Bible into numerous living languages of the earth, elevation of debased tribes, demonstration of the adaptation of the gospel to all

---

* Report of Secretary of State, 1873.

conditions of humanity, contributions to science and commerce, and manifold advantages resulting to the cause of a common Christianity, furnish abundant warrant for gratitude and hope. Even the want of civilization has been no bar to the advancement of the gospel. The modern missionary, equally with the Apostle of the Gentiles, may say, "I am a debtor both to the Greeks and to the barbarians; both to the wise and to the unwise."

"It is the dictate of a wise missionary policy to adapt methods of labor to the varied circumstances of different fields. While the general principles to be observed in the conduct of missionary work may now be regarded as settled, and while the great object of establishing self-supporting, self-propagating churches is kept in view, the application of these principles must be suited to the peculiar circumstances of each race and nation."—*Dr. Clark.*

VII.

MISSIONARY METHODS AND AGENCIES.

THE main principles of missionary policy and action obtain an almost unanimous acceptance. Unity is a marked feature of the movement. Joseph Cook, just returned from a visit to the missions of Asia, was greatly impressed by the union of sentiment among missionaries in Japan, China, and India. "Soldiers who are face to face with the enemy must close up their ranks. The conflict with paganism brings out into the vanguard of the Churches the hidden half of Christian unity." A nobler spirit of catholicity has been amongst the most valuable of reflex results. The Church, while weeping and working for the conversion of the world to Christ, has grown richer in sympathy, more expansive and generous in feeling. This is the *oneness* for which the Redeemer prayed, "that the world may believe that thou hast sent me." Missionaries deeply realize

> "Our fears, our hopes, our aims, are one,
> Our comforts and our cares."

In a "new model of missions," by the late gifted Isaac Taylor, it was proposed to *amalgamate* the several missionary societies. A union of Protestant denominations under one leadership would, it was believed, strengthen and consolidate their work, and enable them to present an unbroken front to the ranks of heathendom. Such a scheme, if at all practicable, might tend to greater uniformity, but scarcely to more of genuine spiritual unity. In the meantime, we are grateful for an almost complete unanimity of thought and action.

Fundamental principles are accepted. It is agreed that all men are sinful, exposed to wrath, and in need of the mercy of God: "because we thus judge, that if one died for all, then were all dead;" that the announcement of "a Saviour, which is Christ the Lord," is for all: "glad tidings of great joy which shall be to all people;" that "the glorious gospel of the blessed God," in its wondrous adaptation, and in the sufficiency of its provisions, meets the varied wants of redeemed humanity, even to the level of the most debased: "a faithful saying, and worthy of all acceptation;" that, by the imperative terms of the Saviour's command, the Church of Christ has been entrusted with the duty of the world's evangelization: "that repentance and remission of sins should be preached in His name among all nations;" that, as the Church at Antioch was required by the Holy Ghost to select and send forth men for distinctively mission work, effort of a costly character must be organized for the universal promulgation of the gospel: "to all them that dwell upon the earth;" that the great promise of this dispensation, "I will pour out of my Spirit upon all flesh," warrants Christian people to pray for and to expect all needed spiritual blessing, and the hastening of the heathen world's salvation.

Missionary methods, based upon accepted principles of spiritual propaganda, should be practicable and sufficiently broad to meet the demands of a universal evangelization.

Questions of method have been frequently mooted. In the first flush of metropolitan popularity, having been invited to preach the annual sermon of the London Missionary Society, the late Edward Irving denounced the modern mission movement. Splendid declamation paved the way to a powerful impression upon popular feeling. A compact organization,—with its board of management, public meetings, and paid agencies,—was said to be a hindrance rather than a help to the progress of the gospel. Machinery was regarded as simply an evidence of the materialism of the age, and of the degeneracy of the Church. Systems were cumbersome. They hampered the cause of evangelization. Modern missionaries, the salaried servants of Societies, subject to specific regulation, were placed in contemptuous contrast with the first messengers of the cross. Apostles of the primitive Church were spoken of as free from human dictation, guided only by the Holy Ghost. In a glowing and impassioned strain, the great orator expatiated on the sublimity of independent action. The true evangelist, according to the preacher's ideal, breaks down every bridge behind him, plunges into the heart of heathenism, trusts to the Saviour for support as well as for success, and leaves a track resplendent with spiritual achievement. It did not seem to occur to the gifted but erratic Irving that it was one thing to go upon such a warfare armed with tongues of flame and the power of working miracles, and another to spend years of toil in the acquisition of unwritten languages, for the means of access to a barbarous people. In the one case there was immediate success to strengthen the soul, and in the other years of patient preparation for a harvest that must be mainly gathered by later reapers. But, in view of modern conditions, the proposal of the preacher was visionary and impracticable. Before we can listen patiently to anything that would seem to discount or depreciate the unselfish and consuming labors of such men as Carey or Judson, Heber or Henry Martyn, Duff or Livingstone, Coke or Calvert, we must be satisfied that there is some more excellent way. In the meantime, grateful for success in the prosecution of ordinary methods, we must seek to lift them as nearly as possible to the line and level of primitive and apostolic work and result.

The subject of "Pauline methods of missionary work," as proposed and pursued by Dr. William Taylor, challenges consideration. It is claimed that the evangelical Churches have largely restricted their religious activities to the multifarious forms and demands of the home work, that they have sent out a comparatively slender force to make known the gospel of Christ to the millions of heathenism, and that our own countrymen resident in foreign lands are largely precluded from the programme of evangelization: "The Churches have but two regular methods of disseminating the gospel. One is by the gradual extension of the home work, and the other is by the authorized location of definite mission fields, the appointment of missionaries, and the appropriation of money to support them, by the regular missionary societies through their officials. Our remote dispersed people are beyond the radius of the first; and not being heathens nor paupers they do not come within the plan or provision of our missionary societies."* In view of the fact that St. Paul and his fellow-laborers, under the direct supervision of the Divine Spirit, aimed at independent organization, and placed the entire responsibility of Church administration upon native converts, it is strenuously urged that missionary Churches and charges should be thrown upon their own resources. In the first days of the Church, Jews were scattered abroad, and became the medium of access to the Gentile populations by whom they were surrounded. Commerce and other exigencies and requirements of modern civilization have thrown English-speaking people upon nearly every distant shore, and it should be the policy of modern missions to utilize that Christian element for the support and diffusion of the gospel among the heathen.

At the Shanghai Missionary Conference, in which

---

* *Pauline Methods*, p. 25.

eighteen of the societies at work in China were represented, "where minor differences were forgotten," and where the simple purpose was to consider "the policy to be pursued and plans adopted for the overthrow of the kingdom of Satan," this question of missionary method and policy came up for consideration. The earlier plan of evangelistic effort in that empire had been to traverse wide spaces of country, preaching the gospel to multitudes. But experience has now taught the laborers of that land to restrict their itinerations, to concentrate working force, and thoroughly to visit a defined district. St. Paul found it expedient to remain three years at Ephesus, and he continued at Corinth for the consolidation of Christian work. The men who know most of China, and who have been eminently successful in their efforts for the spread of the gospel through the eastern part of Asia, find it necessary to repeat their visits, and to "prolong them on each successive occasion."

It may be presumed, where missions differ so greatly in religious character, social status, material resources, and in their immediate surroundings, that no one method can be rigidly or uniformly adopted. Colonial missions planted in communities where language, habits of life, and general conditions are much the same as in England or America, may be made self-dependent at the very earliest stage of their history. There are also missions to mingled communities, English-speaking settlers or traders in the midst of multitudinous forms of semi-civilization, where, through the influences and ascendency of a superior race, a rapid transition should be effected towards self-sustaining organization. But where missions are planted in the heart of heathenism, the conditions are essentially different. Foreign missionaries have to conquer languages, create a literature, translate a Bible, uproot the superstitions of ages, and with their families form the model of a nobler and purer social life.

The question of *self-support* comes to the front of modern mission enterprise. To its fullest extent this principle or policy finds application in every part of the field, and enters into the missionary plans of all the leading missionary societies. Most of the older missions in different parts of the world have been thrown very largely upon their own resources. A series of questions was lately put by Joseph Cook to large gatherings in ten representative cities of Asia. Inquiry had special reference to this subject: " Ought native Christians to be encouraged and instructed to give a tenth of their income to the support of their Churches?" "No, *not yet*," was the reply of many leading and influential minds of the several evangelical bodies. But a few mission-workers, especially of the American Board, said "Yes." "One evening in Bombay I was putting a series of questions to a company of missionaries and civilians, and this question about self-support was among the inquiries. Scotch and English missionaries, one after another, rose and opposed such a pressure as is brought to bear upon native Churches by instructing them to give a tenth of their income for the support of their pastor; but, finally, up rose a converted Brahman from out of the field of the American Board, and, in the most incisive, almost classic English, nearly turned the feeling of the company in favour of the American plan."* The problem of pushing the principle of self-support, and of throwing weighty financial obligations upon native Churches, will doubtless resolve itself in the near future. But "in the beginning of the gospel" there must be communication "concerning giving and receiving."

Missionary methods create and comprise *educational forces and facilities.* Dr. Duff, putting the impress of a commanding mind upon the missionary policy of India, infusing into intellectual enterprise a good measure of his own intense and impassioned feeling, was disposed to put education to the front, and to make it the most evangelistic of appliances. The class-room was to prepare the way for direct access to the heart and conscience of the student. Preachers of the various evangelical denominations, through efforts for individual conversion, would engage "in separating as many precious atoms from the mass" as the stubborn resistance to ordinary appliances would admit, he, by the blessing of God, would "devote time and strength to the preparation of a mine and the setting off of a train" which should one day explode and tear up the structure of Hinduism from its lowest depths. But, on the other side, at the

---

* Monday Lectures, January 29th, 1883.

recent Calcutta Conference, as the result of conviction and experiment, it was urged that the great want of India to-day is preaching. "Education is spreading, breaking down the Hindu faith, and we must preach the gospel to them at this crisis." There is clearly a considerable margin for difference of judgment in regard to guiding policy. What shall be the place and proportion to be assigned relatively to evangelical and educational agency and effort? Unquestionably the original command was to preach or herald the gospel, to make a proclamation of the glad tidings of salvation. The first messengers of the cross could not but feel that their main business was to preach Christ and Him crucified. "So from Jerusalem," said the great missionary of the primitive Church, "and round about unto Illyricum, I have fully preached the gospel of Christ." There was a distinction of spiritual enterprise that could never be set aside in deference to any human device. As a preacher of righteousness, he magnified his office, and counted all things but loss for the excelleney of the knowledge of Christ Jesus. But while the Apostle would not quench a single ray from the light of that sacred story which gathers round the cross, he sanctioned subordinate agency, and gladly utilized each diversity of mental and spiritual qualification and endowment: "For unto one is given, by the Spirit, the word of wisdom; to another the word of knowledge, by the same Spirit; to another faith, by the same Spirit; to another the gift of healing, by the same Spirit;" to others the interpretation of tongues, and other gifts.

Evangelistic methods demand *adaptation*. The main purpose must be, through the process of individual conversion, to secure a purified and elevated national life. But it has been charged that, instead of a civilization suited to the genius and condition of Oriental character and life, missionaries have sought to make English Christians, and in a great measure have denationalized their converts. It was the belief of Bishop Patteson that a mistake had been made in the policy of Protestant propagandism: "Few men think themselves into the state of the Eastern mind. We seek to denationalize those races, as far as I can see." There can be no compromise of the truth as it is in Jesus. But Christianity is a spiritual system. The gospel, as a message of salvation, should not be encumbered with unnecessary social requirements. Native usages of India or China, at all compatible with the spirit and precepts of the New Testament, ought scarcely to be condemned on the ground of being foreign to Western ideas. St. Paul's tolerance of national and race differences suggests a safe principle of missionary action: "Unto the Jews I became as a Jew, that I might gain the Jews; to them that are under the law, as under the law, that I might gain them that are under the law; to them that are without law, as without law (being not without law to God), that I might gain them that are without law. To the weak became I as weak, that I might gain the weak: I am made all things to all men, that I might by all means save some."

Missionary measures and methods should be framed and adopted with a view to *the utmost economy of men and means*. Feeble and scattered efforts do not effectively promote the cause of the world's evangelization. Territory should be distributed. A principle of non-interference should be sacredly regarded, for it subserves the general good and growth of missions. With easily-recognized exceptions, such as centres of population, the several societies may find it expedient to occupy different fields of labor. An admirable report on "Waste in Foreign Missions" was presented on the closing day of the London Methodist Œcumenical Conference. Its suggestions are applicable to the operations of all evangelical missions; and, with such *changes of phraseology* as the adaptation of a larger field demands, it can with advantage be reproduced:

(1.) That any Christian body desiring to take up a new mission field should, if possible, select one not occupied by any other missionary society; or, if the field be large enough to admit of joint occupancy, a portion of the field should be chosen not already occupied by other bodies; or, if the work must necessarily be intermingled, cities and towns not already occupied by other evangelical agencies should be by those proposing to enter; always considering, however, that it may be important to have centres for each body in the capital cities of States and Provinces, and that some cities are of such great population as to admit of joint occupancy. (2.) In case of any trespass, real or imaginary, upon these guiding principles, we advise that the largest measure of forbearance and charity be exercised. Alienation or strife in the presence of those whom we come to save must be exceedingly disastrous. Let each case of alleged interference be fraternally examined by the missionaries, all the considerations be carefully weighed, and a decision reached that shall not be tainted by any selfishness or desire for denominational aggrandizement; solely influenced by pure and noble desires for the greatest glory of our common Master and the greatest good of His kingdom. (3.) That when different bodies of Christians, for any reason have entered the same field, there should be the frankest and most brotherly mutual recognition, and, as far as possible, co-operation. Where this prevails any evils that might possibly arise will be reduced to a minimum, and beneficial influences might even arise from the loving co-existence of the bodies in the same field. (4.) We are not prepared to recommend any general council of reference for the adjustment of such cases. The evils complained of have not assumed such dimensions as to warrant such a proposal; indeed, from an examination of this subject, we think the evil may be far less in extent than is generally supposed, and we must look for the ultimate remedy to the prevalence of the spirit of brotherly-kindness and Christian wisdom among missionaries themselves, and in the boards and committees of directors.*

A noble spiritual unity has been made and manifested in the progress of missions. Exigencies of the hour demand continued co-operation and mutual support. In their simultaneous movement, and in the occupancy of strategic positions, evangelistic forces ought to be a unit. From the world-wide watch towers of effort and aggression, there should roll up an accordant strain: "One Lord, one faith, one baptism, one God and Father of all, who is above all, and through all, and in you all."

Missionary plans must aim at provision for an adequate agency; for the immediate exigencies of particular fields, and for the ultimate evangelization of the whole heathen world.

A comprehensive missionary policy frames measures of reinforcement, and looks well to means for a *continued supply of laborers*. An ordinary method is to train men *in* the work. But should there not be also a training for a special field? Might not the acquirements of returned missionaries be more generally utilized in this department of preparation? Some of us can remember that not a few of the valuable and permanent impressions of life were received from the lips of such honored men, many of whom had hazarded their lives for the Lord Jesus. Memory at this mo-

---

* See *Proceedings of the Œcumenical Methodist Conference*, pp. 587, 588.

ment goes back to an eager group in a north of England-grammar school. The members of that band had been recently converted to God, and were specially susceptible to spiritual impressions. A graphic and glowing description of the work of God amongst dark and benighted races of people moved their souls to missionary enthusiasm; and in more than one case it led to the formation of purpose, and to life-long results. In a course of twelve lectures, the touching and triumphant story of a century and a-half of Moravian mission toil has been recently told to the students of Andover Seminary, and to those of the Theological Department of Boston University. Would it be possible for young men, whose love and loyalty have been plighted to the cause of the Redeemer, without a renewal of holy resolve, to remember such examples of faith and patience, intrepidity and daring achievement? Why should missionary addresses of that eloquent and elevated strain and character be restricted to the students of one or two theological institutions? Ought not the young men of several such colleges, during the formative period of life and purpose, to be made acquainted with the exigencies, claims, and sublime aspects of missionary enterprise? Difficulties do not deter young men of character and purpose from offering themselves for the most arduous fields of toil. George Piercy, in his Yorkshire home, was roused to sympathy for the perishing millions of China, and offered himself for that mission. He was not at once accepted, but such was the strength of conviction and resolve that he disposed of what property he had, sailed to China, studied the language, began a new mission, and then renewed his offer to the church. Now he ranks with the most honored and successful missionaries of the eastern world. Has not Christendom a thousand young men ready for any evangelical enterprise, waiting for a summons to the field and front of action?

It seems strange that, in their influential seats of learning, Protestant denominations have not done more to utilize consecrated Oriental scholarship for the benefit of missions. Roman Catholicism has its Society for the propagation of the faith. The *Collegio de Propaganda Fide*, in Rome, standing on one side of the Piazza di Spagna, founded two centuries and a half ago, was designed by the astute and enterprising Gregory as a retreat for scholars, and a nursery for missionaries. Professors are mostly selected from the staff of mission laborers. Numerous languages are taught. But the instructors are supposed to possess other than linguistic qualifications. They burn with an intense passion for spiritual conquest. An unattractive building is the centre of a world-wide influence. A hundred or more of young men are there under training for the foreign field. Each student, in addition to incidental advantages, obtains an acquaintance with the languages of the civilized or uncivilized lands of heathenism which he expects to use in his future mission. An organized scheme, under evangelical auspices, for turning to account the best services of returned missionaries, might open to us new sources of power and success.

Missionary methods should have regard to *the raising up of a native ministry.*

One of the leaders of Christian work in India has put upon record his sense of the importance of this subject. Were there but two missionaries in his district, we are assured one of them should give his time and strength to the great work of training native agents. It is rightly concluded that in clearing the forests and jungles of heathen superstition, and in preparing the soil to receive the good seed of the kingdom, they must look for native fellers, and also provide for them sharp axes. "What," said a scornful Brahman to a solitary missionary, "you talk about converting India to the Christian religion? It cannot be done! You might as well," he said, pointing to a strip of wood, stretching away to the distance of twenty-five miles, "take an axe and attempt to fell that forest." The pale-faced teacher was prompt in reply. He could do it. "But mark you, every stick I cut will be a handle for another axe, and yet another, until the wood rings with the strokes of the fellers, and every branch shall be lopped off, and every trunk shall be laid low."*

An opportunity was afforded during the visit of Narayan Sheshadri to this country of listening to a cultured Brahmin; a convert to the faith of Christ,

---

*Rev. J. Walton's *Speech*, Exeter Hall, May, 1865.

and an ordained minister of the Presbyterian Church in India. As with flexible expression, and almost faultless diction, he discussed and defined questions and doctrines of science and theology, one could not but feel that through the agency of a native ministry there must be grand possibilities in the future of missions. Accustomed to a tropical climate, independent of the necessities of an European civilization, a native preacher easily adapts himself to all the exigences of the work. There is a vantage ground of immediate access to the heathen mind. He penetrates the reserve of his countrymen. Exposition and refutation proceed from the standpoint of native thought, and they attract by the drapery of fitting and familiar expression. "Oh," said a veteran missionary "there is that in the tones of a foreigner's voice which falls heavy and cold on the ear of a native, whereas there is something in the genuine tones of a countryman's voice which, operating as a charm, falls pleasantly on the ear, and comes home to the feelings, and touches the heart, and causes its tenderest chords to vibrate."*

Any misgiving one might have entertained in regard to the expediency of native agency yields to the logic of facts. Twenty years ago the great Tinnevelly mission of the Church of England had a staff of sixteen European missionaries; but, now, with the exception of the bishop and three educationists, the preaching and pastoral work of eight hundred and seventy-five

---

* *Life of Dr. Duff*, vol. 1st, page 293.

villages devolve upon converted Hindus. A Wesleyan missionary of South Africa attributes the good results of a recent and extensive revival to the earnest manner in which a splendid band of local preachers had worked and striven to bring the heathen to Christ. He avows himself a staunch believer in the employment of native agency, for the purpose of reaching the masses. The converted Zulu has scarcely, it is thought, an equal anywhere in the zeal with which he seeks the salvation of his own people; for soul-saving work is with him an intense and consuming passion, and he exults to gather new spoils to the Redeemer's cross. But no country or race can claim a monopoly of material for an efficient native ministry. What more beautiful character than that of Joeli Mbulu, a Tongan preacher, as delineated by Miss Gordon Cumming, could one expect to meet in any land? "The first to welcome us on landing," speaking of a visit to Bau, "was the native minister, Joeli Mbulu, a fine old Tongan chief. His features are beautiful, his color clear olive, and he has grey hair and a long silky grey beard. He is just my ideal of what Abraham must have been, and would be worth a fortune to an artist as a patriarchal study." Through scenes of cannibalism and dark and horrid practices, for the space of forty years, Joeli persevered in his arduous work, was ordained to the ministry of the gospel, and charged with the oversight of a mission to a separate group of islands. Tongans are naturally a superior race. "Better pioneers could not have been desired. Men of strong energetic character and determination, keenly intelligent, physically superior to the average Fijian, and therefore commanding respect, they had always taken the lead wherever they went; and as in their heathen days they had been foremost in reckless evil, they now threw their whole influence into the scale of good. Foremost amongst these was Joeli Mbulu, a man whose faith is evidently an intense reality." The end of this man was full of peace, a beautiful exhibition of the power of saving and sustaining grace. "The noble face lighted up as we entered, and he greeted us as was his wont—with holy and loving words. He was perfectly calm, and the grand steadfast mind clear as ever." "He was quite conscious to the very last, and the expression of the grand old face was simply beautiful—so radiant as of one without a shadow of doubt concerning the home he was so near." *

Missionary methods ought to aim at provision for *an extension of medical agency.*

It is impossible to ponder the facts of Christ's mission and ministry without marking the prominence which He has assigned to works of healing. The Saviour ministered to the bodies as well as to the souls of men. By a manifestation of compassion He won His way to the hearts of the multitude. "But that ye may know that the Son of Man hath power on earth to forgive sins, He saith unto the sick of the palsy, Arise take up thy bed and go into thy house."

---

* *At Home in Fiji,* pp. 123 and 316.

It was reserved for the American Board to attempt the systematic introduction of medical practice as an auxiliary to direct evangelical agency. Dr. Parker led the way in 1835. His labors were crowned with signal and decisive success. Medical agency, while Christlike and beneficent in itself, can be made to subserve direct spiritual results. To many thousands of those who passed through the hospital of the Canton medical mission the sublime doctrines of revelation were announced and expounded, and thousands of copies of the gospels distributed. An extraordinary tribute to the value and influence of medical missions may be found in the fact that a hospital under native management has been recently opened at Kin Kiang. Chinese officials acknowledge the great good that has been wrought through the agency of Christian physicians; but, in their proclamation, affirm that through hospitals and charitable institutions the foreigners are rapidly stealing away the hearts of the people. Even the *Times*, not remarkable for enthusiasm on the subject of missions, congratulates the missionary societies upon their achievements in this direction. " The combination of the minister to the soul with the minister to the bodily health is not an original, but it is certainly a happy thought. The physican carries in the healing art an infallible letter of introduction. The *penetralia* of an alien religion, and an alien social system, are thrown open to the doctor, whether man or woman." Medical missions offer to the members of a noble profession, glad to consecrate their acquisitions to the cause of the Redeemer, a sphere of valuable service. What course of life is more to be coveted than that of treading in the footprints of Divine and yet human pity and tenderness. The blessed Saviour, moved with compassion, even on His way to Calvary and the redemption of a world, often stayed His steps for the purpose of healing the sick, ministering to the helpless, or for wiping away the scalding tear from the face of some bereaved and sorrowing one.

Missionary methods must assign an important place to *the agency of consecrated Christian women.*

Through the Zenana mission, and its closely related departments of work, the Church has been led along silently and unconsciously to a point where such an instrumentality can be utilized to an almost unlimited extent. A terrible seclusion has been amongst the wrongs which heathenism has inflicted on the women of Oriental lands. The missionary use of the word zenana has mainly reference to the home life of India. It is that part of the house which belongs exclusively to women, and to which they are cruelly restricted. Once it was supposed that life in the zenana had many attractions. There was an idea that a woman " within the gay Kiosk " found much to gratify the sense and to fascinate the fancy:

> "She leads a kind of fairy life,
>   In sisterhood of fruits and flowers,
> Unconscious of the outward strife
>   That wears the palpitating hours."

But the veil has been lifted from the zenana.

Uncounted millions are suffering degradation from inherited pagan customs. Of all the miseries to which human life is subject in this sinful and sorrowing world, there is nothing more pitiable than those of the immured daughters of India. The fact is keenly realized. Many a mother would welcome death for her daughter, rather than the wretchedness of a life to which she seems irrevocably doomed. There is nothing to soften the barbarity of exclusion. No ray of brightness or gladness ever reaches or relieves the interior of the dungeon dwelling. Mind is manacled. The noblest part of nature remains undeveloped, and the best capabilities of the soul are dwarfed. "Ignorance," said a Hindu lady bitterly, "is the ornament of women in our land." Life in the zenana has no resources for alleviation or comfort. Existence is a dull and dreary monotony. In case of sickness, or of epidemic disease, there is frequently a frightful and a fatal neglect. Such are the inexorable customs of a Hindu home, that a skilful physician cannot see his moaning and helpless patient, feel her feverish pulse, or make himself acquainted with her actual condition. There can be no communication except through the medium of a slave; but an attempt has been made, successfully, to penetrate the gloom of the prison-house, to open the doors to them that are bound. Christian ladies from western lands, with requisite medical training, find access to the curtained recesses of the zenana. As angels of love and mercy, the women sent out from our Churches fulfil a sorely needed ministry to their sorrowing sisters in India. They hold in their hands the key of homes and hearts. "I believe," says Dr. Valentine, "the female medical missionary will relieve an amount of human suffering that lies beyond the reach of any medical man, and bring to a knowledge of the truth those that are shut out from any other form of human agency." Thousands, through this means, have heard tidings of the great Healer and Helper of human souls, and their hearts have pulsated with a new-found gladness. One hundred million of woman to be reached by the zenana missionary! What a field for loving labor!

"Before their dumb idols the prisoners are falling;
Vainly, alas! to their gods do they cry;
With helpless hands lifted to you they are calling,
O sister come over and help us ere we die!
Come over and help us, come over and help us;
O sister, come over and help us ere we die!"

"O why," wondered a Hindu woman, "have I not heard of this before? Why has no one come to tell the women of my province?" Wasted by long sickness, she heard of one that had come from a far-off land to heal the sick, and to help the sufferer. The "foreign lady" was in another province, but re-action from hopelessness brought strange strength. By a great effort she reached the plains below. As the medical missionary smoothed with soft touch her fevered brow, counted her fitful and fluttering pulse, she whispered in her ear the story of Jesus and His love, of the Saviour's mission to earth, and of the home of many mansions. The weary one found refuge and peace. But her latest plea, before passing away to be with the Lord, was for yet unvisited heathen homes: "Won't you send some one up among the hills to tell these sweet words to the women of my province?"

The Macedonian cry 'of the zenana finds a noble response. One after another, ladies of refinement and culture leave their attractive homes, renounce the charms of social life, and go out to that distant land for the purpose of ministering to the sick, caring for the dying, blessing the little children, and of guiding wandering and weary ones to the Redeemer and Helper of human souls. A gifted English authoress, A. L. O. E., for the sake of this needed ministry of love, has renounced large emolument and high literary anticipations. Another accomplished lady, Lucille H. Green, made a like sacrifice. She had taken her degree from the College in Philadelphia, and prospects were all bright for a successful career at home. But all gifts were laid at the foot of the cross. The pine-clad hills of New Jersey were exchanged for the strange scenes and tropical plains of Hindustan, and for the hospital with its dusky occupants. She "sang her way across the sea;" and, in anticipation of many hours of lonely watching, sought and found needed strength in the assurance of the Saviour's promised presence:

> "That holy Helper liveth yet,
> My friend and guide to be;
> The Healer of Gennesaret
> Shall walk the rounds with me."

Unmarried ladies, having obtained a competent medical education, are sent out to the East by various societies; and, in some cases, private means enable them to go out at their own expense. By a single mail steamer, a few months ago, eight ladies from America landed at Bombay. They were unattended by gentlemen, and proceeded the same day to Allahabad. From that city on the Ganges they would separate, some going to Calcutta, and others to the north-west. The growing extent of this work is simply astonishing, and is rightly regarded as a remarkable sign of the times. "If any one had said to me, twenty-five years ago," writes that veteran of Indian missions, Mr. Leupolt, "that not only should we have free access to the natives in their houses, but that zenanas would be opened in cities like Benares, Lucknow, Agra, Delhi, Amritsir, and Lahore, and that European ladies with their assistants would be admitted to teach the Word of God to them, I would have replied, 'All things are possible to God, but I do not expect such a glorious event in my day.' But what has God done? More than we expected and prayed for."*

---

* Quoted by Dr. Christlieb from "Church Mission Intelligencer," *Foreign Missions*, p. 10.

"It is easy to feel a generous glow, while we sing in the words of Heber,—

> 'Waft, waft, ye winds, the story,
> And you, ye waters, roll.'

But listen! The winds are sweeping, and have been sweeping from the beginning over the peaks of the Himalaya, and on the shores of Lake Tsad. Now it is the rustle of the breeze, now the shock of the tempest; but listen? Does either sound on the ear the name *Jesus?* The waves are rolling, and from the beginning have been rolling, on the shores of Fiji and Japan; but does either the gentle ripple or the boom of the mighty wave, sound the word *mercy?* No; if the story be told, *it must be told by the voice of living men.*"
—*Wm. Arthur.*

VIII.

GO, OR SEND: THE COMMISSION.

"AND Jesus came and spake unto them, saying, All power is given unto me in heaven and in earth. Go ye therefore, and teach all nations, baptizing them in the name of the Father, and of the Son, and of the Holy Ghost: teaching them to observe all things whatsoever I have commanded you: and, lo, I am with you alway, even unto the end of the world. Amen."

The last command of Jesus was definite and supreme. There could be no difficulty in regard to interpretation. Had the commission been inscribed on an angel's flaming scroll, and renewed from age to age, it could not have been more clearly traced. The parting words of the Saviour were to disciple all nations; to go into all the world, and preach the gospel unto every creature; to be witnesses in Jerusalem, and in all Judea, and in Samaria, and unto the uttermost part of the earth.

The designation of Saul of Tarsus to an apostolic mission was also explicit: "For I have appeared unto thee for this purpose, to make thee a minister and a witness both of these things which thou hast seen, and of the things in the which I will appear unto thee; delivering thee from the people, and from the

Gentiles, unto whom now I send thee, to open their eyes, and to turn them from darkness to light, and from the power of Satan unto God, that they may receive forgiveness of sins, and inheritance among them which are sanctified by faith that is in me."

At Antioch in Syria, where missionary enterprize was first organized, a line of action was clearly marked out for the future guidance of the Christian Church: "As they ministered to the Lord, and fasted, the Holy Ghost said, Separate me Barnabas and Saul for the work whereunto I have called them. And when they had fasted and prayed, and laid their hands on them, they sent them away. So they, being sent forth by the Holy Ghost, departed unto Seleucia; and from thence they sailed to Cyprus."

Mission work demands strong men. Preachers of commanding power and eloquence, the most prominent men of the Church of Antioch, were selected as pioneers of the gospel in new lands.

The first missionaries did not act upon their own responsibility. They returned to Antioch for the purpose of reporting results. "And when they were come, and had gathered the Church together, they rehearsed all that God had done with them, and how he had opened the door of faith unto the Gentiles." A most important principle was then recognized. There was to be no isolation of the foreign from the home work.

Under the direction of the Holy Ghost, the Church prayerfully set apart efficient men for new and arduous enterprize; and, in sending them away, fervently recommended them to the grace of God for the work they were expected to fulfil.

The Saviour's final command is the charter of Christian missions, and the action of the Church in Antioch furnishes an infallible precedent for missionary appointment. Gospels and Acts are mutually explanatory. The commission, as Divinely interpreted, means

"GO, OR SEND."

From such an order there can be no safe deviation. Less than this would not suffice for the exigencies of evangelistic enterprise. By what agency shall the message of salvation be borne to the world's perishing millions? Night and day the Church hears a sorrowing Macedonian appeal. Shall that wail of weary anguish pass by unheeded? The great heart of humanity throbs in response to a glad evangel. But "how then shall they call on him in whom they have not believed? and how shall they believe in him of whom they have not heard? and how shall they hear without a preacher? and how shall they preach except they be sent? as it is written, How beautiful are the feet of them that preach the gospel of peace, and bring glad tidings of good things!"

The mission of the apostles was to begin *from* Jerusalem. The first proclamation was made from beneath the very shadow of Calvary. Home missions first of all! But even then the universality of the gospel dispensation was made apparent. Parthians, and Medes, and Elamites, and the dwellers in Mesopotamia, and in India, and Cappadocia, in Pontus, and Asia, Phrygia, and Pamphylia, in Egypt, and in the parts of Libya about Cyrene, and strangers of Rome, Jews and proselytes, Cretes and Arabians, heard in their own tongue the wonderful works of God. Other sentiments have at times been propounded. " Charity begins at home !" " The Greeks are at our own doors !" Aphorisms and sarcasms have been frequently appealed to and perverted for mean and selfish purposes. " We have no religion to spare," was the contention of a member of the Massachusetts Legislature, in opposition to a measure for the incorporation of the American Board of Missions. There was a fear that " if too much of the precious commodity were sent away they would be impoverished at home." But the reply in substance was, that such was the nature of religion, the more they gave away the more they had. Exportation to the perishing ones of foreign lands did not exhaust, but tended to the increase of, home religion and resources.

When the evangelical enterprise of the Baptist Church, in the early part of the century, began to blaze out into a splendor that caught the wondering eye of Christendom, many good people feared that the movement would lead to denominational depletion. " I think it my duty," said a prominent minister of the body, in the exercise of editorial influence, " to crush this rising missionary spirit." But he lived to see that fears were groundless, and that a new epoch in the diffusion of Christianity had been auspiciously inaugurated.

There is only one line of action by which the Church of Christ can be led along to ultimate and assured strength and success. Were she to cease from spiritual enterprize the glory would depart. Missionary movement does not resemble a mountain stream, where by repression a slender rivulet may be swollen to a strong torrent. It is rather analogous to flame; and, by being pent up, a fire may be extinguished. "The very soul of our religion is missionary, progressive, world-embracing; it would cease to exist if it ceased to be missionary, if it disregarded the parting words of its Founder."*

The commission has never been revoked. But very slowly has the Christian Church realized the weighty significance of the charter with which she has been entrusted. Sense of duty was long enwrapped in mist and haze. The first attempt of William Carey to interest his brethren in the subject of missions was a failure, and was met by a mortifying rebuke. He was told to sit down, and assured that when God was pleased to convert the heathen it would be done without his aid. But that is just what the Lord does not do. A consecrated human agency is demanded for the diffusion of the gospel. The tongue of fire, and not an archangel's trumpet, is the emblem of an appointed ministry. "And all things are of God, who hath reconciled us to himself by Jesus Christ, and hath given to us the ministry of reconciliation; to wit, that

---

* Max Müller "On Missions," *Ecl. Mag.*, p. 260.

God was in Christ reconciling the world unto himself, not imputing their trespasses unto them; and hath committed unto us the word of reconciliation."

The question of duty to the heathen world came up, in 1796, for discussion in the General Assembly of the Church of Scotland. Modern mission schemes were denounced as visionary, " highly preposterous," and as a sign of the restlessness of the times. Revolutionary tendencies, it was feared, lurked in proposed forms of united action, and the very constitution of the church might be imperilled in such a movement. Who were they, that they should attempt to interfere with redeeming plans, or the purposes of God? Ought they not rather to wait in patience and in prayer? Nor could they hope to turn the myriads of India from the superstitions and habits of ages. Civilization must precede Christianity. It was not to the dark and barbarous hordes of Africa and India, but to the polished cities of Corinth and Rome, that St. Paul directed his footsteps. Such was the reasoning of men whose only business in life was to preach the gospel. The commission was apparently ignored, and a strong feeling of hostility to missions developed. But the spirit of one evangelical leader in that memorable debate was moved to an intense and irrepressible emotion. " Moderator," said Dr. John Erskine, who seemed for the moment to have caught the fire of some commissioned prophet or apostle, " *rax* me that Bible!" Christ's supreme command was thrillingly emphasized, and the effect was as that of lightning from a clear sky. The assembly was brought back to first principles, and the law of the kingdom was searching to heart and conscience. An unfavorable resolution was adopted. But already the current of feeling had begun to turn, and an adverse vote could never be repeated in the courts of the Scottish churches. A new and nobler era of missionary enterprise was near at hand. "It was indeed a token that better days had come for the Church of Scotland, when Chalmers and Duff were contemporaneously making the whole country resound with their noble pleadings—the one for the heathen at home, the other for the heathen abroad." *

Even yet the force of the Saviour's command can scarcely be said to have struck home fully to the heart of the church. The weight of responsibility is only measurably realized. Resolve and effort do not rise to the level of solemn obligation. Many a Macedonian appeal sweeps past unheard or unheeded. "Did the church really believe the gospel to be as necessary to the heathen as to us, there would be an end of guilty repose. It would be easier to find rest in our beds over the throes of an earthquake. The agonies of Laocoon and his children, dying in the coils of a serpent, were but pastime compared with those of the church, until she had either unlocked herself from the grapple of the conviction, or disburthened her conscience by the faithful consecration of her energies to the work of rescuing the world from its doom."†

---

* *Life of Dr. Duff*, Vol. 1st, p. 301.
† Dr. Olin's *Works*, Vol. 2nd, p. 385.

To go, means denial of self. The spirit which this cause demands is that of supreme abnegation. A device, said to have been copied from an ancient monument, an ox standing between plough and altar, with a suggestive legend, *ready for either*, has been adopted for the official seal of an influential Society. The genuine missionary gives himself without reserve, for service or sacrifice, doing or suffering, life or death. An ideal of consecration finds expression in hallowed resolve:

> "Ready for all Thy perfect will,
> My acts of faith and love repeat;
> Till death thy endless mercies seal,
> And make the sacrifice complete."

Missionary annals abound with examples of highest heroism. The first messengers of the cross, when charged with fanaticism, went on in their glorious enthusiasm, saying, "For whether we be beside ourselves, it is to God." Bound for the dark East, Francis Xavier knew not what things might befall him there, and an impassioned utterance burst from his lips. A night vision passed before him. Millions of fellowmen were perishing, and he longed to rush to their rescue. But there was a fearful ordeal of trial to be undergone. One was scourged, another stoned, and others committed to the flames. Would he brave all that peril for the sake of preaching the gospel to the heathen? The zeal of the intrepid missionary was as a mighty flame in his soul, and he cried out, "Yea Lord, yet more! *yet more!*"

It would be easy to multiply examples of resolve and endurance. What deed of earth can better claim an immortal record than that of the youthful Moravian, who voluntarily became a slave for the sake of securing access to the slaves of the West Indies? Appointed to the island of Jamaica, a mission to the negroes on the plantations, he found the door closed. A prohibitory Act had passed the local Legislature, making it a serious crime for any person to attempt the religious instruction of the slave population. But the heroic missionary could not abandon the project. He sold himself into bondage. The humiliation must have been keen, but an opportunity was won of whispering a message of salvation to unrequited children of toil, and indignity was glory in disguise. Scars in the service of the Redeemer are a badge of distinction. That slave brand was highest honor:—

> "Than its traces never yet,
> On old armorial hatchments, was a brighter blazon set."

In the earlier days of missions, a young girl of the United States read of a remarkable work of God in Burmah, and was fired with the thought of service for Christ. "And I, too," was the resolve, "yes I too will be a missionary to the heathen." But, for a time, life took another direction. "Fanny Forester" became a star of the literary firmament, and won both fame and fortune. Then came a genuine surprise. A whisper went out, indistinctly at first, afterwards confirmed, that this favorite of society was to become the wife of a distinguished missionary. The proposal was met by an indignant protest. Had the full chalice of popular applause been offered in vain? That one who shone with such distinction in circles of wealth and fashion should be sacrificed to the cause of missions, and be borne off to grim Burmah, was deemed an outrage upon taste, culture, and refinement. "Does she deem that stern duty calls her to resign the home and friends of her heart, the fame which she has so gloriously won, nay, more, perhaps even life itself, for the sake of the far-off heathen?" But, in repudiation of the charge of "madness," throwing away her splendid gifts, she pointed out the folly of those who were spending their lives in the pursuit of earthly pleasure, and exulted to lay "laurels and life" at the Redeemer's feet. Cost was counted. Her father would never wait again for his daughter's coming tread. She was to be regarded as with the dead. But there was the hope of re-union in a land of life and love,—

> "Not sorrowing then as now,—
> She'll come to thee, and come, perchance,
> With jewels on her brow."

For missions the Church needs the very best men at her disposal. The first and indispensable requisite for this work is an intense missionary impulse. There should be a burning passion for the salvation of souls. Consecration must be complete. "A live coal," says the prophet, "was laid upon my mouth." Isaiah's lips were touched with hallowed flame. Iniquity was taken away, and sin was purged. Sanctity was meet preparation for service. "Also I heard the voice of the Lord, saying, whom shall I send, and who will go for us." Communion with God renders the soul responsive to such an inquiry. The air is full of voices that men and women in their worldly moods do not hear. The Prophet would not have heard the Divine call in the temple, nor St. Paul the Macedonian cry on the Ægean coast, had not the attitude of the soul been one of reverential solicitude. There can be but one answer to sacred appeal: "Here am I, send me." There must be no transfer of responsibility. A specially qualified and summoned messenger of salvation may not plead, as Moses was tempted to do at the burning bush, "O my Lord, send I pray Thee by whom Thou wilt send." Should there be any lack of enthusiasm? "As My Father hath sent Me," the Saviour said, "even so I send you." We have been accustomed to think of that Divine mission as one of solitary grandeur; and yet for each toiler, baptized into the same mind, there is something of a like greatness in reserve. A mission to save souls, possibly to wreathe the Redeemer's royal diadem with an added splendor, is enough to make even the fiery pulse of an apostle beat into a deeper sympathy: "Unto me who am less than the least of all saints is this grace given, that I should preach among the Gentiles the unsearchable riches of Christ."

It was observed in reference to a graduating class

of one of the United States denominational colleges, comprising seventy students, that only seven entered the ranks of the Christian ministry—one-tenth of a band of young men "not undistinguished by native gifts and literary acquirements." A very large number of intellectually-gifted young men, pledged to the cause of Christ, enrolled in the membership of the Church, are passing through the halls of various universities. An abundant agency ought to be available for all the exigencies of the home and foreign work. For such a ministry, angels might willingly exchange their thrones of light. Missionary consecration is the demand and hope of the hour. The Master calls, and the world waits.

Qualities of a high order are required for efficiency and success. The men for this enterprise must be as those that went with Saul to Gibeah, "a band of men whose hearts God had touched." It is a glorious thing for the Church when young men of Christian families, educated at the best seats of learning, endowed with intellectual gifts that might win distinction and applause at the Bar or in the Legislature, possessed of a business capacity which ordinarily may command success in a commercial sphere, impelled by sense of duty and constrained by the love of Christ, turn aside from the attractions and emoluments of professional and mercantile life, and, seeing a hand that others do not see, hearing a voice that others do not hear, pledge all the possibilities of redeemed being upon the altar of a high and hallowed purpose.

THE COMMISSION. 223

It was a privilege in earlier life, having offered and been accepted for the foreign work, to associate with a number of youthful missionaries on the eve of embarkation for a foreign shore.* They had been summoned to meet the Missionary Committee in London, with a view to an immediate appointment. From different parts of the British Isles these young men came together at the Centenary Hall in London. An hour was spent in prayer. How vivid the remembrance of that day, and of that scene! If ever the Divine promise, "Lo, I am with you," was memorably fulfilled to God's missionary servants, keenly sensitive to accepted responsibilities, it was then. The place seemed full of holy influence. Vows of consecration were renewed, and needed help was earnestly implored. Destination had not been determined. Few of the number had any certainty in regard to appointment. The field was the world, and the laborers stood ready to enter at any point. In one case the son of an esteemed Wesleyan Minister was named for Sierra Leone. The station up to that time had proved exceedingly fatal to European missionaries, and was regarded as a land of death, or "the white man's grave.' There was a perceptible shadow upon his fine countenance as he came back from an interview with the members of the committee. "Well, brother," the

---

* Medical examination in the case of the writer, it was understood, influenced an appointment to the bracing climate of North America, rather than to the enervation of tropical heat.

usual question as each returned to the room, "what is your appointment?" It was not what had been anticipated, nor the most congenial to feeling, but an unrestricted offer had been made, and he could not find it in his heart to intimate any sense of reluctance. It must be of God. This gifted and esteemed missionary was able to say what many others felt, "But none of these things move me, neither count I my life dear unto myself, so that I might finish my course with joy, and the ministry which I have received of the Lord Jesus, to testify the gospel of the grace of God." After a brief course of two years on the western coast of Africa, he caught the contagion of fatal fever, and was laid to rest in the mission graveyard. By the earliest steamer, or sailing ship, others of that company voyaged away to distant spheres of toil; to Newfoundland and the West Indies, to West and South Africa, to Ceylon and continental India, to Australia and the Islands of the Southern Pacific.

The question of duty ought not to be left to the consideration of any one class of workers in the mission field. A Divine command crosses the path, or lies along the line, of every life. To every man according to his several ability is the law of obligation. No special ordination is requisite to the fulfilment of soul-saving work. Openings for usefulness constitute a providential call to the needed ministry. It has often been felt, especially in India, where British Christianity is represented by thousands of civilians, that an insufficient influence has been exerted for the promotion of spiritual enterprise. Not solitary was the remark of an Indian Colonel, returning home in company with a respected Missionary, that during a long residence in the East he had never witnessed a native conversion; but he could tell of notable hunting exploits, and of rare deeds in forest and jungle. But then the clergyman, after spending as many years beneath the same burning sky, and with much experience of travel, had never seen an elephant shot. The retort was to the purpose, and the officer could only confess that the ordinary path of his life had been away from scenes of spiritual effort.

A decided change, however, has become apparent in recent years. The roll of Christian workers in the great British dependencies includes honored names from each department of the public service, and from the ranks of business men. As the motto of a commonplace book, on his way out to the Civil Service of India, Alexander Brown adopted a stanza from Robert Browning, written after passing St. Vincent. A line was underscored:

"Here and here did England help me,
How can I help England?"*

It is a noble thing to face colonial life as the representative of a great nation, concerned for the best social interests of the people, and not from a mere

---

* A. Brown, early departed, was the gifted son of Dr. David Brown, the eminent Exegete of Aberdeen.

mercenary motive, or the greed of commercial gain. But it is a still more laudable thing to take a step in advance of patriotism, and to live unto Him who died for us and rose again. To many a man whose lot is about to be cast in a new land, an important question may lie outside the range of personal consideration. How can I best help these settlers or aborigines of the colony? By what means can I aid the work of God in Japan or China, in Australia or Africa, to which business may bind me for years or for life? Shall I not accept a commission from the Church, enroll my name as a member of some pledged band of Christian workers, and thus become an acknowledged witness for Jesus?

Have we not a right to expect new departure in missionary enterprise? The time may not be far distant when, with deepened sense of obligation, and abundant facilities of travel, business and professional men shall plan an occasional visit to the great mission field. Incidental aid could be adjusted to the studied flexibility of missionary organization. A few weeks or months of such service might prove to be of incalculable advantage to a struggling charge, an aggressive movement in some populous heathen city, or in an attempt to break ground on a new soil.

We can think also of another possibility of the missionary future. Candidates for the ministry, at or near the close of a collegiate course, and prior to the accepted responsibilities of home work, may deem it a duty and a privilege to spend a few months or years on a mission station. Robert Murray McCheyne was all the more fitted for settlement in Dundee when, in the spirit of sanctified resolve, he made the record of readiness for a foreign field: "I am now made willing, if God should open the way, to go to India; here am I, send me." "My missionary race was short," says William Arthur, of the Mysore Mission. "God made it so. But, looking back this day, I would not for the universe have the brief space blotted out of my existence."

Our children should be early imbued with a missionary spirit. Many Christian men and women, with this cause upon their hearts, are unable to enter a foreign field. They are bound by indissoluble ties. But may they not do a great work, through the dedication of their children to the Lord's service? At twelve years of age, Hannibal of Carthage was sworn upon the altar of his gods, and the vow of eternal enmity to Rome breathed its spirit into a life of relentless and indomitable purpose. Youthful decision has often been influenced at the most critical moment, and character shaped, from the consciousness of parental solicitude. There need be no hesitancy in regard to sacrifice of feeling. No higher honor could the Saviour confer than in claiming our children for the noblest work of earth.

The missionary addresses of Dr. Duff, after his return from India, were urgent in appeal to Christian parents. He demanded, in the name of the Master, the consecration of Scotland's most gifted sons and daughters. Allusion was made, on one occasion, to the steadfast loyalty of a Highland father or mother. One only son had been cheerfully given up to the royal cause, soon probably to find a gory or grassy bed on a wild moor or in some lonely glen. "But, oh, had I ten, they would follow Prince Charlie." That was the unswerving attachment to the unfortunate House of Stuart. What, then, does the cause of Christ demand? Shall Christian parents grudge their children to the service of the King of kings? Before the General Assembly, 1867, a most impassioned appeal was made for the sustentation of missions. Overcome by exhaustion, Duff fainted on the platform, and was carried out to an adjoining vestry. "I was making a speech," he said—coming to and wondering for a moment where he was—"let me go back. I must speak or die in the effort." The missionary veteran, with massive brow and long white hair, tremulous with emotion, stood once more before the immense audience, and received an expression of homage that gold could not have purchased. The vast congregation rose up as one man, and many eyes were wet with tears. A responsive chord was touched in the orator's final appeal: "Fathers and mothers of Scotland, is it true that ye will not let your sons and daughters go to preach the Gospel? I spent twenty-five years of my life in India, lost my health, and have come back to die. If it be true, I will be off to-morrow, and let the heathen know that if I cannot live for them, I can die for them."

Appeal is sustained by an adequate incentive. Earthly aim sinks into insignificance in comparison with redeeming interests. Missionary motives are of the most inspiring and exalted character. By the cross and passion of the blessed Redeemer, the greatness of Mediatorial purpose, the thrill of appeal at the altar of consecration, a deepening conviction of the grandeur of that cause to which we have avowed our allegiance, the unspeakable worth of redeemed and immortal souls, the solemnities of judgment and eternity, we are summoned to ponder the fact of obligation. If the Spirit of Jesus be in us, can we hesitate? A converted native of Burmah was asked to go as a religious teacher to a warlike tribe, where the salary would not be more than a fourth of what was paid to him as boatman. "No," was the reply of Shapon, "I could not go to the Bghai for four rupees. But *I can do it for Christ.*" Was not the guiding principle of that missionary offer a true one? "Worthy is the Lamb that was slain to receive power, and riches, and wisdom, and strength, and honor, and glory, and blessing."

If to *go* for Jesus means much of sacrifice, there shall be an abundant compensation. One aspect or result of mission work has to be kept ever in view. It brings a joy all its own. "I heard you speak about heaven, last night," said an Ashanti convert to a Wesleyan Missionary. "When I go there, I'll go up to my Saviour, and fall down on my knees before Him, and thank Him for having sent a missionary. Then shall I go back to the gate, and wait till you come; and then I shall take you by the hand, and bring you up to my Saviour, and say, *There is the first man that showed me the way to the cross of Christ.*" Such a thought may have been present to the mind of Henry Martyn; as, on the fly-leaf of a Persian New Testament, afterwards found with a converted Mohammedan at Shiraz, he wrote, "There is joy in heaven over one sinner that repenteth."

The missionary receives an assurance of final award. "And Jesus said unto them, Verily I say unto you, That ye which have followed me in the regeneration when the Son of man shall sit in the throne of his glory, ye also shall sit upon twelve thrones, judging the twelve tribes of Israel. And every one that hath forsaken houses, or brethren, or sisters, or father, or mother, or wife, or children, or lands, for my name's sake, shall receive an hundred fold, and shall inherit everlasting life."

"Realize to your own mind the nature of Christian dedication, and the claims of Him who calls for it, and so far from giving penuriously to His cause, you will take every increase of your substance into His presence and devote it to His praise; you will regard every appeal which is made to your Christian benevolence as an appeal to that solemn treaty which made you His, and you will honor it accordingly; you will deeply feel the penury of all riches as an expression of your love to Him."—*Dr. John Harris.*

IX.

MISSIONS AND MONEY.

A PROBLEM of money confronts the Church. Humanly speaking the question of the world's evangelization is one of ways and means. How shall adequate missionary funds be obtained? Do Christians rightly recognize the duty and privilege of giving for the support of the Lord's cause? Obligation is universal.

Religious liberality is a subject of sacred inculcation. The Jew, under the Theocracy, was bound by enactment to give a tenth of his increase to the service of the Lord. A second tenth had to be held sacred for the support of the great national festivals. Once in three years a third tenth seems to have been levied for the poor of the land. It has been computed that a Hebrew householder contributed from a fifth to a third of his income to religious purposes. There was one law that could admit of no exception: "And ye shall eat neither bread nor parched corn, nor green ears, until the self-same day that you have brought an offering unto your God: it shall be a statute forever, throughout all your generations, in all your dwellings."

Still there was reserved a generous margin for freewill and other offerings. A splendid liberality was exhibited by the Church in the wilderness, and substance without stint brought to the treasury of the Lord. "And they came both men and women, as many as were willing-hearted, and brought bracelets, and earrings, and rings, and tablets, all jewels of gold: and every man that offered, offered an offering of gold unto the Lord." A proclamation that giving must cease had to be made throughout the camp. "So the people were restrained from bringing. For the stuff they had was sufficient for all the work to make it, and too much." Repeated is the record of sanctuary liberality: "Every one offered a freewill offering unto the Lord." "As for me," said Salem's greatest king, amassing treasures for the building of a temple, "in the uprightness of mine heart I have willingly offered all these things: and now have I seen with joy thy people, which are here present, to offer willingly unto thee." The same principle demands expression under the gospel dispensation: "Freely ye have received, freely give." "For if there be first a willing mind, it is accepted according to that a man hath, and not according to that he hath not." "Every man according as he hath purposed in his heart, so let him give; for the Lord loveth a cheerful giver." "Remember the words of the Lord Jesus, how he said, it is more blessed to give than to receive."

Spontaneity imparts aroma to the sacrifice. Alexander of Macedonia filled both hands with rich perfumes, and threw the costly offering upon the altar. Profuseness of expenditure in the service of the gods was believed to be the surest pathway to success, and to the accumulation of treasure. Should Christians be penurious in the presentation of their altar gifts? Is it possible to imagine the meanness of counting grains of incense lest a particle too much should go to the sanctuary offering? "I have no pleasure in you, saith the Lord of hosts," as the people stinted their gifts, "neither will I accept an offering at your hands." A nobler era, of a distinctive missionary character, must be inaugurated. "For from the rising of the sun to the going down of the same, my name shall be great among the Gentiles; and in every place incense shall be offered unto my name, and a pure offering: for my name shall be great among the heathen."

Liberality tends to increase, not to impoverishment. "Honor the Lord with thy substance, and with the first-fruits of all thine increase: so shall thy barns be filled with plenty, and thy presses shall burst out with new wine." "With what measure ye mete it shall be measured to you again."

A period of utter selfishness, in the history of the Church, has ever been marked by spiritual dearth. The people of a corrupt age kept back their gifts from the altar. Indignant was the tone of Divine expostulation. "Will a man rob God? Yet ye have robbed me. But, ye say, wherein have we robbed thee? In tithes and offerings." An occasional demur at the demand of gold for the Gospel might suggest another inquiry: Will God rob a man? Does the great Lord of all require anything in excess of our means? Are not God's people challenged to the test of generous gift? "Bring ye all the tithes into the storehouse, that there may be meat in mine house, and prove me now herewith, saith the Lord of hosts, if I will not open you the windows of heaven, and pour you out a blessing that there shall not be room enough to receive it."

Once, in this matter of religious liberality, an experiment was made in the Church. The result was marvellous. Deficit had been the ordinary condition of temple finance. Now there was an abundance. Tithes accumulated. The treasury overflowed. Every avenue of distribution began to be choked. Ministers were called to account for the immense surplus. "Then Hezekiah questioned with the priests and Levites concerning the heaps. And Azariah the chief priest of the house of Zadok answered him, and said, Since the people began to bring their offerings unto the house of the Lord, we have had enough to eat, and have left plenty; for the Lord hath blessed his people: and that which is left is this great store."

The teachings of Inspiration are explicit in regard to methods of giving for religious purposes.

Apostolic direction was given to the Churches of Galatia and Corinth: "Upon the first day of the week let every one of you lay by him in store, as God hath prospered him, that there be no gatherings when I come." This was what Paley understood to mean as being "charitable upon a plan." An objection should be anticipated at the outset of this explication. It may be claimed that St. Paul had reference to matters of temporal relief, not to the duty of giving for the support of missions. But does not the principle of this injunction apply palpably to every purpose of Christian liberality? Specific statement lifts the subject far above the level of a local or incidental arrangement. The epistle was addressed not only "unto the Church of God which is at Corinth," but "to them that are sanctified in Christ Jesus, called to be saints, with all that in every place call upon the name of Jesus Christ our Lord, both theirs and ours."

Contribution must be *general:* "Every one of you." This order was according to a former legal enactment: "None shall come before me empty." Small amounts swell the aggregate. Mites make millions. It is a noble thing when the Arthingtons and McArthurs of the old land, and equally generous contributors of our own country, in proportion to their abundance, give princely sums to the treasury of the Lord. But the gifts of the lowliest are not to be undervalued. Once in temple teaching, Jesus "sat over against the treasury." A deed of devotion which he there beheld won the tribute of special recognition. "Many that were rich cast in much." But there was one woman, with a care-worn and patient expression, shrinking from public gaze, that quietly dropped a small coin into the chest. Such gifts were of scant account in the estimation of sacerdotal treasurers. That unobtrusive act was unheeded of men, but it was approved of God.

The Saviour looked to the priceless love that prompted the lowly offering, and gift and giver were immortalized. "And he looked up and saw the rich men casting their gifts into the treasury. And he saw also a certain poor widow casting in thither two mites. And he said, Of a truth I say unto you, that this poor woman hath cast in more than they all: For all these have of their abundance cast in unto the offerings of God: but she of her penury hath cast in all the living that she had."

He who spoke approvingly of the widow's mite would not slight the gifts of childhood. "Every one of you" must include the younger members of the family. "The children gather the wood," is the suggestive record of an ancient idolatry, "and the fathers kindle the fire, and the women knead the dough to make cakes to the queen of heaven." All kinds of service were utilized. Upon a like principle should the Christian Church secure youthful sympathy to the cause of missions. Sabbath-schools ought to be saturated with facts of gospel progress. The offerings of nearly thirteen million of scholars, even on the average of a cent a month, should form a valuable addition to the missionary fund.

Giving to the cause of God should be *systematic:* "On the first day of the week." Such a service constitutes an act of worship. The day of the Redeemer's resurrection is hallowed throughout the Christian world. Hearts are constrained to reverential love. The Lamb that was slain is worthy to receive *riches.*

On the Lord's day the claims of the Lord's treasury are to be sacredly remembered. To some business men, the giving of money seems nearly related to secular concerns, and is regarded as an intrusion upon the sense and sacredness of Sabbath devotion. They would fain exclude all allusion to finance from the sanctuary service. There is felt to be a taint of worldliness in the mere fact of enforcing the duty of giving for religious purposes. But such a feeling, less common now than formerly, springs from a defective view of Divine requirements. Consecration to the service of the Lord admits of no reserve. The altar sanctifies the gift. Sabbath influence hallows the offering. Lowly members of the Church, priests by virtue of a heavenly calling, minister of their substance unto the Lord. The incense of a grateful heart accompanies the sacrifice, and wafts its fragrance to the skies. Nothing is reserved. Substance and service are alike offered to God. The prayer is—

"Take my silver and my gold,
Not a mite would I withhold."

Giving ought to be *proportionate:* " As God hath prospered him." It may be convenient, in dealing with the statistical aspects of the subject, to speak of averages. *But proportion and not average is the doctrine of Scripture.* Jacob set up his memorial at Bethel ; and, by a solemn vow, bound himself to a covenant God : " Of all that thou shalt give me, I will surely give a tenth unto thee." A later direction was explicit :

"They shall not appear before the Lord empty : every man shall give as he is able, according to the blessing of the Lord thy God which he hath given thee." The tithe, as we have seen, the proportion of increase, was a law of the Jewish economy. "To every man according to his several ability" is the principle of Christian obligation. Give as God hath prospered you. But is there not some statute of limitation ? Shall we find it in the New Testament ? The first note sounded in the gospel is that of good-will to men. "You are surrounded by an atmosphere of fervent joy and love ; solicited by a feeling of which the deeds are every good work, distributing, communicating, making sacrifices with which God is well pleased ; stimulated by examples of Apostles forsaking all, individuals selling all, Churches bestowing all, the deeply poor giving to the poorer, and the Master giving always, storing never ; and in the end giving Himself a ransom for all."*

Motives to liberality in contribution are numerous and urgent.

In the Second Epistle to the Corinthians various aspects of this subject are explained and enforced. Affectionate and earnest are the pleadings and exhortations of the Apostle. The spirit of inspired inculcation belongs to all ages.

Christians of the primitive Church were encouraged to keep up *the standard of liberality.* A good beginning

---

* William Arthur on *Giving*, p. 110.

had been made at Corinth. The impulse of Achaian deeds had been felt by distant communities. Macedonia was a mission. A great trial of affliction had tested the faith and steadfastness of the converts. But a gracious stimulus had been received; and, with limited means, they stood ready to help to the full measure of their ability. "The abundance of their joy and their deep poverty abounded unto the riches of their liberality. For to their power I bear record, yea, and beyond their power, they were willing of themselves; praying us with much entreaty that we would receive the gift, and take upon us the fellowship of ministering to the saints." That Macedonian record has been repeated in the history of modern missions. Facts of native contribution often put to shame the stinted gifts of settled and wealthy home Churches.

The Saviour's example furnishes a *supreme incentive*: "For ye know the grace of our Lord Jesus Christ, that though he was rich, yet for your sakes he became poor, that ye through his poverty might be rich." How hearts thrill beneath the touch and power of that appeal. Many a time as the ages have rolled along, has it raised the flood-gates of generous sympathy. Never can we be insensible to the power of the Redeemer's cross and passion:

"Love so amazing, so divine,
Demands my soul, my life, my all."

There should be an assurance of *equality* in demand and privilege: "For I meant not that other men be eased, and ye burdened. But an equality, that now at this time your abundance may be a supply for their want." It was expedient that even an Apostle, in his urgent plea, should furnish the fullest explanation of the transaction. Missionary managers can always afford to take their constituency into the most complete confidence. A law of proportion is to be observed in demand and distribution. Native Churches and congregations must bear their share of financial burdens. An efficient administration aims at equality. But the exhortation has another purpose. Souls are perishing. Millions are destitute, famishing for the bread of life. Jesus had compassion on the multitude. Shall not something of the same solicitude and yearning pity for mankind move the heart of the Christian Church? Think of the erring and benighted ones, whom Christ died to save, and Christians are commissioned to succour! They range over western prairies—roam over Russian and Tartar steppes—crowd the banks of the voluptuous Ganges—stretch out their hands from Afric's sunny and sorrowing lands—wait wearily in the distant Isles of the Sea. Is it nothing that we are permitted to take part in the work of amelioration, and of salvation? Not for all the gold in every earthly mine would an earnest Christian man or woman forfeit the right to a ministry of love and mercy. There is equality of privilege. All may have a share in the glorious enterprise. The smallest labor is not lost. No gift prompted by love to the Saviour, and placed at His feet, seems large or small. The pierced hand of Jesus receives and hallows each offering. Yes, there is an "equality!"

As an encouragement to generous contribution, there was *a guarantee of economical disbursement.* The Apostle would not personally undertake the administration of church finance, or the management of this special fund. No suspicion of self-interest must shadow or diminish the force of earnest appeal and of a faithful ministry. But the work was to be entrusted to a thoroughly competent brother: "whose praise is in the gospel throughout all the churches; and not that only, but who was also chosen of the churches to travel with us with this grace which is administered by us." In regard to ability and integrity there was every ground for confidence. This point touches a general principle or question of missionary finance. Administration must be competent. It is a boon to any Society to secure men for its executive that command unbounded confidence; and it does seem that special qualification accompanies designation to office in this department of church organization. A fear has sometimes been expressed that contributions to missions cost too much to carry them to their destination. But a "little arithmetic" applied to the treasurers' statements, as furnished in the annual accounts of the various societies, dispels the doubt, and removes the ground for any shadow of imputation. "It is a very simple thing to find the percentage of expense, and we know no surer or more convincing answer than for any doubter to investigate for himself."

Contributors to the relief fund of the early church were encouraged to expect *a good and sure return for their liberality.* "But this," says the Apostle, as the exponent of a law which applies in full force to the duty of giving for the support of missions, "He which soweth sparingly shall reap also sparingly; and he which soweth bountifully, shall reap also bountifully." Assurance was given that, as their substance was freely bestowed, God would make all grace to abound toward them; that, "having all sufficiency in all things," they might "abound to every good work." Return was sure. They could not sow in such a soil without the security of an ample harvest. "Now he that ministereth seed to the sower, both minister bread for your food, and multiply your seed sown, and increase the fruits of your righteousness."

Christian liberality promotes *the glory of God:* "For the administration of this service not only supplieth the want of the saints, but is abundant also by many thanksgivings unto God." This argument applies also to the missionary enterprise. A characteristic transition leads the mind up to the eternal throne. Service promotes praise. From forest and prairie choirs, redeemed tribes of Africa, groups of Chinese worshippers, bands of Hindu converts, as the result of missions, a rapturous strain ascends to heaven. Each day enlarges the concert, and augments the song. How valuable the sacrifices and services of the saints! A burning seraph might covet the privilege of adding a grain of incense to the fragrance of pure and hallowed offerings. But the generosity of an earthly giver is only a reflection and result of Divine munificence: "Thanks be unto God for his unspeakable gift."

Missionary contribution demands an immediate augmentation.

Sanctified liberality has already exhibited many a triumph over human selfishness. The penuriousness of the Christian Church, in a former time, was keenly felt by thoughtful men. "Truly," said Lord Bacon, "merchants shall rise up in judgment against the princes and nobles of Europe; for the merchants have made a great path in the seas, unto the ends of the world, and have sent forth ships and fleets of Spanish, English, and Dutch, enough to make China tremble; and all this for pearl and stone and spices. But for the pearl of the kingdom of heaven, or the stones of the heavenly Jerusalem, or for the spices of the Spouse's garden, not a mast has been set up." But the missionary movement has been as the smiting of the desert rock; it has unsealed fountains of Christian liberalty.

The stream of evangelistic enterprise, traced to its source, generally leads up to some spring of pure and practical beneficence. At the Leeds Conference, 1769, when Wesley deputed Boardman and Pilmoor to the pioneer work of spreading the gospel in America, a collection was made towards the expenses of the new mission. The organization of the Kettering Baptists, 1792, was signalized by a financial effort. Independents at Warwick, in the formation of a missionary society, followed the example of their Wesleyan and Baptist brethren. Modern missions, at their birth, were baptized by the spirit of liberality. Such contributions may seem small to us, but, from what we know of the originators of this work, they must have represented a good deal of self-denial. Each decade, however, marks a large increase in the scale of giving for the support of missions. From a quarter of a million, at the commencement of the century, the missionary income now reaches the annual sum of eight million of dollars; but, in view of urgent need, the amount ought to be at once doubled and trebled. The Church might then multiply her agencies, and prepare for the work of a universal evangelization.

Missions need money. Could there be a more legitimate appropriation of surplus funds? Even the coinage of heathen Greece was stamped with the emblems of religion. The Roman mint adjoined the temple. Should not hoarded treasures of our time be placed under contribution for the Lord's service? Resources are ample. Christian nations have abundance of gold in their vaults. Do you doubt it? Are not rich mines of the earth, wealthy corporations, and the commerce of the world, under their control? Five hundred million dollars, the net gain on a year's productions, was the amount added in 1882 to the capital of the United States. A tithe of this store would replenish the mission treasury. Talk of depletion! Giving, as a rule, has not yet been carried up to the point of self-denial; and, until the tide of religious liberality shall flow in a deeper channel, or sweep on with a swifter current, we may not expect to see the reign of millennial glory.

Can any one reasonably object to the *cost* of missions? Compare the outlay with the expenditures of extravagance. It is a matter of statistical truth that "the drink bill of Great Britain and the United States alone is $1,450,000,000 a year—with twice as much as the cost of the traffic." An English general election costs the political parties of that country nearly as much as the aggregate of annual expenditure for all the missionary societies in the world. Trade returns of the American Union include one hundred and twenty-five million dollars for such goods as silks and laces, twenty-five million for kid gloves, and five million for ostrich feathers. Wealthy members of Churches are known to expend large sums in fashionable entertainments. "We are told of weddings costing tens, and even hundreds, of thousands of dollars." Easter floral decorations, in the superb ecclesiastical structures of three or four large cities, are said to cost two hundred thousand dollars, and all for a perishing beauty and fragrance. How much in proportion ought to be paid for the announcement of a risen Saviour to the waiting nations of the earth? One million of dollars, according to the *Herald*, is spent by the excursionists of New York on a single Sunday; and the cost of theatres and kindred amusements, to the pleasure-seekers of the same city, is put down at seven million a year. Christian penuriousness, brought into comparison with the lavish expenditures of luxury and pride, becomes absolutely appalling to serious thought. Acts of generous liberality obtain a suitable record; but a solemn and sorrowful truth needs none the less to be flashed upon the conscience of the Church. While mammon's altars are burdened with costly offerings, and votaries of pleasure waste their gold, the cause of the Redeemer languishes for lack of the means that his followers could well afford to give." "I gave my life for thee," is the appeal from Calvary; "what hast thou given for me?"

Facts of heathen liberality, with which missions bring us into contact, have in them a promise and potency of better things. Life and treasure are held subject to the gods. A million of dollars has been received in offerings, largely from the poor, at a single Hindu festival. One form of idolatry costs China a hundred and fifty million dollars a year. Rich Brahmans and Buddhists expend immense sums for the increased magnificence of their temple worship. Shall not wealthy Orientals, with their splendid ideas of giving for worship, one day bring their contributions for the service of the world's Redeemer? Eastern worshippers opened their treasures at the Saviour's birth, and "presented to him gifts; gold, and frankincense, and myrrh." Converted natives of the East, thronging to the mountain of the Lord's house, may yet lead the van of missionary liberality. "Then shalt thou see and flow together, and thine heart shall fear and be enlarged; because the abundance of the sea shall be converted unto thee, the forces of the Gentiles shall come unto thee. The multitude of camels shall cover thee, the dromedaries of Midian and Ephah; all they from Shebah shall come: they shall bring gold and incense."

> "Thy rams are there,
> Nebaioth, and the flocks of Kedar there;
> The looms of Ormus, and the mines of Ind,
> And Saba's spicy groves, pay tribute there."

Shall Christians grudge their money for missions? Dr. Livingstone believed that the time would come when, instead of profuse expenditures for pride and luxury, rich men would count it an honor to support whole stations of missionaries. A late merchant prince of New York, of revered name and memory, made his business tributary to religion, and was accustomed to forecast with a view to probable appeals. "I have found my ability to give," he said, " somewhat largely the greatest luxury of my life. The money is laid by, the call comes, and I am not tempted to the baseness of inventing excuses." An esteemed Ohio doctor prayerfully set apart a tenth, and then a fourth of his income to the Lord's cause. A written pledge, found since his death, covenants that the principal of his fortune should not be allowed to exceed seventy thousand dollars; and, as the Lord blessed him with means "beyond what he had expected or desired," the aggregate gifts for special religious purposes amounted to over five hundred thousand dollars.

Missionary munificence knows no maximum. It is regal after the manner of Araunah the Jebusite: Did he not "as a king give unto the king?" Sacred promise must be regarded as equivalent to supreme command: "I will consecrate their gain unto the Lord, and their substance to the Lord of the whole earth."

"The days, O brethren, roll rapidly on, when the shout of the isles shall swell the thunder of the continent; when the Thames and the Danube, the Tiber and the Rhine, shall call upon Euphrates, the Ganges, and the Nile; and the loud concert shall be joined by the Hudson, the Mississippi, and the Amazon, singing with one heart and one voice, 'HALLELUJAH! SALVATION! THE LORD GOD OMNIPOTENT REIGNETH!'"—*Dr. John M. Mason.*

"Come then, and, added to thy many crowns,
Receive yet one, the crown of all the earth,
Thou who alone art worthy!—
Receive yet one, as radiant as the rest,
Due to thy last and most effectual work,
Thy word fulfilled, the conquest of a world."
—*Cowper.*

X.

THE WORLD FOR CHRIST.

CHRISTIANITY is not a mere wave on the restless ocean of human thought. The allegiance of the world belongs to Jesus. Essential majesty is the Redeemer's most radiant crown. It was his before the world was, ere the white wing of the first created angel had stirred the pure ether of illimitable space, even from everlasting. But a diadem of mediatorial right has also been purchased by the Saviour's cross. The very thought of regal triumph is full of rapture, and there is ample warrant for anticipation. Every purpose connected with the exaltation of the Lord Jesus demands an ultimate and acknowledged supremacy: "For to this end Christ both died and rose and revived that he might be Lord both of the dead and living." The world for Christ! Is not the expectation a legitimate one?

Missionary anticipation is sustained by an accordant strain of sacred prediction.

> "Sweet is the harp of prophecy; too sweet
> Not to be wronged by a mere mortal touch:"

But, though under the restraint of such a thought, an attempt may be made to unfold the significance of the prophet Isaiah's opening vision.* "And it shall come to pass in the last days that the mountain of the Lord's house shall be established in the top of the mountains, and shall be exalted above the hills; and all nations shall flow unto it." The temple of ancient worship, central to all lands, becomes, in this prophetic scene, the type and precursor of a future spiritual glory. Gleaming and elevated spires strike the wondering vision from afar, and the courts of the Lord's holy house are thronged with worshippers. Natural conditions and tendencies, as in the case of magnetic force, or of water under the power of gravitation, are reversed, and a living tide of humanity flows up from the nations, into the Church of God.

"And many people shall go and say, Come ye, and let us go up to the mountain of the Lord, to the house of the God of Jacob: and he will teach us his ways, and we will walk in his paths: for out of Zion shall go forth the law, and the word of the Lord from Jerusalem." Illumination shall be universal. In the eighth century, when darkness was dense, St. Benedict dreamt that he beheld the whole dark world lightened by a solitary sunbeam. That which was

---

* "It is a common but erroneous impression that the missionary spirit is almost entirely the product of the new dispensation, and that not much of it is to be found in the old. If such were really the case, the cause of missions would lose the aid of one of the most powerful principles that now lie at its foundation. We can but advert, in passing, to the further development of this principle in the writings of Isaiah."—*Church of England Magazine.*

only a beautiful vision to the Italian saint shall be ultimately realized;

> "The beam that shines from Zion's hill
> Shall lighten every land;
> The King who reigns in Salem's towers
> Shall all the world command."

"And he shall judge among the heathen," continues the prophet, in expansion of the mediatorial idea, "and shall rebuke many people, and they shall beat their swords into ploughshares, and their spears into pruning hooks." A superb painting by Salvator Rosa, in one of the great galleries of Florence, indebted to inspiration for the magnificent conception, exhibits "peace burning the implements of war." In a measure the prediction has had a missionary accomplishment. Hostile and warring tribes, bent on the extermination of their foes, delighting in burning and bitter feud and animosity, have been known to exchange their murderous weapons for the implements of industrial pursuit. Converted South Sea islanders have been seen to remove the barrel of the musket from its stock, place it on the anvil, and beat it out into a spade or hoe for the cultivation of the soil. The smooth and polished rails of the stairway leading to a very plain-looking pulpit, in one of the most spacious sanctuaries in the southern Pacific, affording accommodation to fifteen hundred people, was literally formed of spear handles, stained in many a sanguinary struggle.

Luminous and lofty prediction also announces the final overthrow of error, and the ultimate result of spiritual aggression. Does the Church need encouragement, and the strength that springs from assured success? A glorious promise gleams on the inspired page: "And the Lord alone shall be exalted in that day. And the idols he shall utterly abolish. In that day a man shall cast his idols of silver, and his idols of gold, which they made each one for himself to worship, to the moles, and to the bats." The eternal God declares that the heathen nations shall forsake their gods, and that the idolatries of the earth shall be utterly overthrown. This is a wonderful thing. Even the destruction of one idol, around which superstitious feeling has closely gathered, as the climbing ivy around some crumbling ruin, is a great achievement. When, throughout the Roman empire, the overthrow of paganism was resolved upon, a stately temple of Serapis in Alexandria was doomed to destruction. It was one of the most magnificent structures of heathenism, and the idol was of immense proportions. It was announced by the priests that whoever injured that temple or insulted the god would rouse seven-fold thunders, and cause heaven and earth to return to their primeval chaos. To a people steeped in idolatry, an assault upon the deified occupant of that stately shrine could not be thought of without a tremor. But a stalwart soldier planted a ladder against the image, struck a vigorous blow with his axe, and broke the spell of superstition.

Thunder was silent. No burning bolt visibly scathed the audacious assailant. A spirit of iconoclasm took immediate possession of the multitude. The dumb, impotent idol was hewn to pieces and dragged in triumph through the city.

The destruction of Serapis, in the queenly city of the Nile, signalized a victory for the Christian faith. Such trophies abound. It would not be easy to enumerate the heathen deities that have fallen before the cross, as Dagon before the ark of God. Isis and Osiris, Molech of Amnon and Chemosh of the Moabites, Jupiter and Minerva, turbulent divinities of the Olympian heaven, "false gods of Hellas," Parthenon and Pantheon, Thor and Woden of Teutonic worship, have sunk into utter oblivion. At one time the idolatries of the world formed an apparently impregnable entrenchment. "See if there be such a thing: hath a nation changed their gods?" But the potent illusion has been dispelled. The carved magnificence of classic antiquity has gone to dust and ruin, to the moles and the bats. Oracles are dumb, altars forsaken, and the lips of old mythologies forever sealed.

> "No more at Delos or at Delphi now,
>   Or e'en at mighty Amnon's Lybian shrine,
> The white-robed priests before the altar bow
>   To slay the victim and to pour the wine,
> While gifts of kingdoms round each pillar twine.
>   Scarcely can the classic pilgrim, sweeping free
> From fallen architrave, the desert vine,
>   Trace the dim names of their divinity;
> Gods of the ruined temples, where, O where are ye?"

Where? Have not these gods, that made not the heavens and the earth, perished from under the heavens? And so must it be with all the idols and superstitions of heathen worship. "Bel boweth down, Nebo stoopeth!" Sabianism and Soofeeism are yet to be superseded by the true light. Mosque and pagoda await transformation into Christian temples. Crowns of Brahma and Buddha shall be laid at the feet of the Divine Redeemer.

The bright page of prophecy must become a brighter page of history. It may not be expedient to determine dates. Accomplishment is the only adequate exponent of sacred prediction. But there ought to be no indifference to inspired utterance. The subject is fraught with encouragement. Ancient promise had reference to heathen nations, as well as to Jewish people: "It shall come, saith the Lord, that I will gather nations and tongues; and they shall come and see my glory. And I will set a sign among them, and I will send those that escape of them to the nations, to Tarshish"—Spain, "Pul"—Asia, "and Lud"—Africa, "that draw the bow, to Tubal"—Russia, "and Javan"—Greece, "to the isles afar off"—Britain and Oceanic islands, "that have not heard my fame, neither have seen my glory; and they shall declare my glory among the Gentiles." "As truly as I live, saith the Lord, all the earth shall be filled with the glory of the Lord." "And the glory of the Lord shall be revealed, and all flesh shall see it together, for the mouth of the Lord hath spoken it." "They shall not hurt nor destroy in all my holy mountain, for the earth shall be full of the knowledge of the Lord, as waters cover the sea." "And the ransomed of the Lord shall return, and come to Zion with songs and everlasting joy upon their heads: they shall obtain joy and gladness, and sorrow and sighing shall flee away." As the pillar of cloud and flame led the way of God's people, in their march through the wilderness, an abiding pledge of covenant faithfulness, the brightness of sacred prediction streams along the track of evangelical enterprise; and, as an advancing banner of light, inspired promise leads the van of the missionary host.

The testimony of Jesus is the spirit of prophecy. Messianic themes glow with all the rapture of missionary anticipation. "For unto us a child is born, unto us a son is given: and the government shall be upon his shoulder: and his name shall be called Wonderful, Counsellor, The mighty God, The everlasting Father, The Prince of Peace. Of the increase of his government and peace there shall be no end." "Ask of me," was the covenant stipulation, "and I shall give thee the heathen for thine inheritance, and the uttermost parts of the earth for thy possession." Universal empire in a worldly sense is a dream and delusion, but the Lord Christ shall have an enduring supremacy. "I saw in the night visions, and, behold, one like the Son of man came with the clouds of heaven, and came to the Ancient of days, and they brought him near before him. And there was given him dominion, and glory, and a kingdom, that all people, nations, and languages, should serve him: his dominion is an everlasting dominion, which shall not pass away, and his kingdom that which shall not be destroyed."

Apostles are in full accord with the goodly fellowship of the prophets. Some of the most magnificent passages of the New Testament have reference to the regal glory and final triumph of the world's Redeemer. The head that once was crowned with thorns is crowned with glory now. "That ye may know what is the hope of his calling, and what the riches of the glory of his inheritance in the saints, and what is the exceeding greatness of his power to us-ward who believe, according to the working of his mighty power, which he wrought in Christ when he raised him from the dead, and set him at his own right hand in heavenly places, far above all principality, and power, and might, and dominion, and every name that is named, not only in this world, but in that which is to come; and hath put all things under his feet, and gave him to be head over all things to the Church, which is his body, the fulness of him that filleth all in all." The Saviour claims the homage of a redeemed world. "Wherefore God hath highly exalted him, and given him a name which is above every name: that at the name of Jesus every knee shall bow, of things in heaven, and things in earth, and things under the earth; and that every tongue should confess that Jesus Christ is Lord, to the glory of God the Father."

The trend of providential movement is palpably in the direction of inspired prediction.

The outlook is encouraging. Conditions are favorable. Avenues are open. Mission watch-fires multiply on the distant mountain-tops. The inspiration of hope is the strength of the Christian Church. Banners of the sacramental host blaze with the light of conquering resolve. Signs of the times exhibit an extraordinary coincidence. Providential and preparatory movements pave the path to onward achievement. Angels of light and love lead the way. Omnipotence is on the side of militant saints. A power not of earth has brought about changes that tend to the furtherance and triumph of the gospel. "This is the Lord's doing; it is marvellous in our eyes." If, as has been eloquently suggested, superhuman agencies had been employed, all would have admired and bowed down before such a revelation of the purpose of providence. Had heavenly legions been commissioned to minister visibly on the earth, to remove political hindrances, to open up highways to the isles of Japan and of the sea, to the heart of China, to the centre of Africa, the world and the Church would have been awed and constrained to wonder and reverential praise. But Divine interposition has been none the less real, because the way is in the sea, the path in the great waters, and the footsteps not known. "Bulwarks of ages have fallen down. The interior of continents not long ago largely unknown to geography are at this time open to missions. Events not arranged of men have opened all lands to religious truth." Has not God been manifestly leading his people? "He hath shewed his people the power of his works, that he may give them the heritage of the heathen."

During the earlier decades of this century, the burden of missionary prayer was wont to be that God would open doors, break down barriers, divide the seas, dry up the rivers, and prepare a way for the heralds of salvation. All regions of the globe are now accessible to the Bible and the missionary of the cross. Can we doubt that the march of providential movement has been made to subserve the great work of the world's evangelization? The multitudinous thoroughfares of the Roman empire, and the spread of the Greek language, heralded and prepared the way for the triumphs of Christianity in the apostolic age. Art and science,—spanning continents, forming pathways across the billowy deep, encircling the earth with a network of wires, utilizing steam and the mysterious forces of electricity,—the growing power of commerce and civilization, and the genius and enterprise of the time, are aids and allies of the missionary movement, eminently favorable to the progress and diffusion of the gospel:

"Out of the shadows of night
The world rolls into light;
It is daybreak everywhere."

The question of measures and means for the world's evangelization has now to be seriously considered.

A proposition of such immense interest and importance as that which relates to the universal diffusion of the gospel demands patient and prayerful thought. The subject should be pondered in the light of ascertained fact. Mathematical faith is not missionary faith. The problem of the world's salvation has its "unknown quantity." We live under the dispensation of the Spirit, and when required conditions are met, the most sanguine anticipations may be exceeded in the bestowment of promised blessing. But the project must be viewed, on one side, from the standpoint of human agency and appliance. Is the subject a feasible one? What is demanded, in the way of men and means, for the immediate undertaking of such an enterprise? The question was under consideration at the meeting of the Evangelical Alliance, in 1873. Dr. Angus thought it to be demonstrable that with fifteen thousand missionaries at work for ten years, and with fifteen thousand pounds sterling to support them, the gospel might be preached repeatedly to every man, woman and child on earth. Fifteen thousand missionaries! Does the proposal startle the leaders of evangelical movement? Is the demand beyond the resources of the Church? A great country, leading the van of the world's civilization, for the vindication of national honor, the conquest of a single fortress, or the occupancy of a narrow strip of territory, sends as many men to the field and front of battle. Abyssinian, Afghan, and Egyptian expeditions have a voice for the Church. They speak eloquently in regard to effort, endurance, and heroic self-sacrifice. There was never a hesitation on the part of England's noblest sons. For the service of sovereign and country, brave warriors have stood ready to pour out their blood like water, and to follow their colors on distant or perilous enterprise. Surely, for the advancement of redeeming purpose, the spiritual conquest of a world, there can be no difficulty in regard to needed reinforcements! Then

> "send ten thousand heralds forth,
> From east to west, from north to south,
> To blow the trump of Jubilee,
> And peace proclaim from sea to sea."

Fifteen millions sterling for ten years! The amount would about equal the annual interest paid by two or three leading States of Europe on the aggregate of their national debt. Think of it in comparison with the enormous cost of the liquor traffic to the people of Great Britain and the United States! The wealth of any one or two of the leading evangelical denominations, if freely and fully consecrated to the Lord, would amply suffice for every demand, and the missionary treasury could fear no depletion. *An average contribution of twenty-five or thirty cents a week from the communicants of the Methodist Church, in the United States and Canada, would alone go far to meet financial exigencies.*

---

* An article from the pen of Dr. Burns, of Hamilton, in the October and November numbers of the *Canadian Methodist Magazine*, 1883, is well calculated to rouse the slumbering conscience of the Church, and to promote "a missionary revival."

Immediate requirements can be measurably determined. For the successful achievement of the work proposed, one ordained missionary ought to be sent out for every fifty thousand of the accessible population of the heathen world. The people yet to be reached by the gospel may be estimated at seven hundred millions, and thus fourteen thousand missionaries must be added to the staff of foreign laborers. Then it is claimed that if the Churches would give a dollar to missions for every five they expend on themselves, the message of salvation could be carried to every heathen dwelling, and the Bible put into the hands of every son and daughter of the human race. "I plant myself on these propositions," says Joseph Cook, "which I believe have the approval of great secretaries of missions—one missionary for every fifty thousand of the accessible pagan population of the world; one dollar to be expended for missions for every five expended for ourselves." *

A prominent writer on modern missions pleads for the summoning of an Œcumenical Council, solely to plan for a world-wide spiritual campaign, and to mature measures for bringing the glad tidings of salvation into contact with every human soul in the shortest possible space of time. It is believed that the world could be evangelized in twenty years, and that before the close of this nineteenth century the

---

* The Vanguard of Christian Missions, Monday Lecture, January 29, 1883.

gospel of the Redeemer might be given to every living soul. The estimate of agency in this case is exceedingly moderate. "At least ten thousand more missionaries" are needed. "Let the field be mapped out and divided, with as little waste of men and means as may be; let there be a universal appeal for workers and for money, a system of gathering so thorough that every giver shall be regularly brought into contact with the Lord's treasury." *

The views of eminent exponents and advocates of this great project, so far as they have been adduced, are found to be in substantial agreement, and their estimate of required agency sufficiently near for all practical purposes. The bare suggestion of such an achievement is enough to stimulate interest, strengthen faith, deepen the fervor of prayer, arouse expectation, and afford encouragement to continued and increased effort. Were capitalists or business men to contemplate a scheme of national or international magnitude and importance, no matter how enormous the proposed expenditure, they would be expected to accomplish it long before the end of the century. No difficulty would be regarded as insurmountable. Funds would be forthcoming, and the globe rapidly girdled with a far-reaching enterprise. Shall the Church of Christ hesitate to pledge herself to magnificent achievement, or to plan for the world's salvation, and the universal extension of the Redeemer's kingdom? Should not

---

* The Gospel in all Lands, Oct., 1881.

the grandeur and greatness of missionary enterprise fill every heart, furnish incentive to unwearied effort, and inspiration to hallowed resolve? "For Zion's sake will I not hold my peace, and for Jerusalem's sake I will not rest, until the righteousness thereof go forth as brightness, and the salvation thereof as a lamp that burneth." "The world for Christ" must become the watchword of a host. "Set up the standard toward Zion." "Lift ye up a banner." The broadest, brightest, loftiest banner of earth bears the blazon of spiritual conquest. Then let it be fearlessly displayed. Give it to the Church. Entrust it to the Sunday-school. Unfurl it from the pulpit. Bear it to every land. Fling it abroad under the whole heavens. "And all the ends of the earth shall see the salvation of our God."

Missionary accomplishment must precede the second Advent. "And the gospel of the kingdom shall be preached in all the world for a witness unto all nations; and then shall the end come." The meaning of the Saviour's important utterance has been well brought out by an apposite illustration. There is a blessed sense in which the gospel shall be a "witness" to the world. The metropolis of Scotland, in 1842, made magnificent preparation for the reception of royalty. Enthusiasm was unbounded. There was a scene then witnessed by thousands, and long after remembered. In Bible times they were required to "set up a sign of fire in Beth-haccarem;" and so on this memorable occasion, as twilight deepened into night, from hill and height around the proud northern city, there was a sudden and simultaneous blaze of splendor. The noble Frith of Forth was all at once illuminated. Beacons and torches flashed their light from Berwick to Stirling. That burst of brightness was well understood. It was a token, a *witness*, to all the people. The Sovereign was at hand. "So shall also the coming of the Son of Man be." Signals of salvation are to be lighted in every land. Mission watch-fires shall be a sign to all the dwellers of the earth. "The gospel must first be published among all nations."

Plans for the world's evangelization should be accompanied by prayer for the world's conversion.

Efforts for enlightenment and evangelization come within the range of human agency and responsibility. But the salvation of the world's multitudes is the work of God, and can only be effected through the energy of the Holy Ghost. Hence the necessity of prayer! Continuity of supplication has been predicted. "Thus saith the Lord of hosts, It shall come to pass that there shall come people, and the inhabitants of many cities: and the inhabitants of one city shall go unto another, saying, Let us go speedily to pray before the Lord, and to seek the Lord of hosts; I will go also. Yea, many people and strong nations shall come to seek the Lord of hosts in Jerusalem, and to pray before the Lord." There shall be a world-wide circle of prayer, a universal embassy to the throne of Omnipotence. Christendom shall be suppliant at the feet of Jesus, and "for him shall endless prayer be made."

The Saviour taught his followers to pray that God's name might be hallowed, his kingdom come, and his will be done in earth as it is in heaven. The prayer, "Thy kingdom come," in which we ask for ourselves and all others the blessings comprised in the diffusion of the gospel, and the universal reign of Christ, is thoroughly and purely missionary in its character and application. As a cloud of incense, that breathing of desire rises from the lips of tens of thousands of assembled worshippers. One could not help feeling during the first week of 1883, as in many former years, that the most characteristic part of the programme was mainly an expansion of the great missionary petition. Christian people throughout the world were asked to unite in prayer for all missionaries and others engaged in mission work, that they might be filled with the Holy Spirit, and that great success might crown their efforts; that all native Christians might be kept steadfast in the faith, and made earnest and efficient in bringing souls to the Saviour; that many more faithful laborers might be called and sent out by the Lord of the harvest; that the Mohammedans and heathens might be won to Christ, and that the Jews might be constrained to receive him as the long-expected Messiah. Repeated request can know no exhaustion. It shall continue to ascend to the throne of the heavenly grace, and to unseal fountains of spiritual blessing, until the utmost of inspired anticipation shall have been realized: "And the kingdom and dominion, and the greatness of the kingdom under the whole heaven, shall be given to the people of the saints of the Most High, whose kingdom is an everlasting kingdom, and all dominions shall serve and obey him."

In prayer for the salvation of men and the conversion of the world to Christ there should be an intense realization of the Holy Spirit's essential office, as the quickener and regenerator of human souls. The great promise of God must be the dependence and hope of the Church: "And it shall come to pass afterwards, that I shall pour out my Spirit upon all flesh." Scarcely had the Redeemer ascended to the mediatorial throne when the baptism of fire was received. Waiting suppliants were crowned with tongues of flame. The sword of the Spirit, bathed in the lightnings of heaven, pierced thousands to the heart. "And fear came upon every soul: and many wonders and signs were done by the apostles." Through dependence upon God, the struggling Church renewed its strength: "And when they had prayed, the place was shaken where they were assembled together; and they were all filled with the Holy Ghost, and they spake the word of God with boldness." The first preachers of the cross avowed the ground of their sufficiency and success: "For our gospel came not unto you in word only, but also in power, and in the Holy Ghost, and in much assurance." This is still the dispensation of the Eternal Spirit. The first call for united and universal supplication, it will be remembered, was for "the effusion of the Spirit of God upon all the churches and upon the whole habitable earth." Every measure of missionary success is due to the gracious influence of the Holy Ghost, and he alone can make the gospel effectual to the salvation of men. It is still with the preacher of righteousness as with the prophet in the valley of vision: "Thus saith the Lord God: Come from the four winds, O breath, and breathe upon these slain, that they may live." Unaided human agency cannot achieve success: "Not by might, nor by power, but by my Spirit, saith the Lord of Hosts." "Until the Spirit be poured upon us from on high, and the wilderness be a fruitful field, and the fruitful field be counted for a forest."

Prayer has to do with movements that subserve the progress and ultimate triumph of mediatorial purpose and administration. A beautiful passage of the Apocalypse indicates an intimate connection between united prayer and the revolutions of earth: "And another angel came and stood at the altar, having a golden censer; and there was given unto him much incense, that he should offer it with the prayers of all saints upon the golden altar that was before the throne. And the smoke of the incense which came with the prayers of the saints, ascended up before God out of the angel's hand. And the angel took the censer and filled it with fire of the altar, and cast it into the earth: and there were voices, and thunderings, and lightnings, and an earthquake." Imagery comes from ancient sanctuary service. As the worshippers bowed in prayer, at the morning and evening sacrifice, priests ministered at the golden altar. Fragrance blended with petition. Incense and prayer ascended together. Thus it is in the ministry of our Great High Priest. The prayers of his people, if earnest and sincere, are mingled with the merit of an atoning and efficacious sacrifice, are hallowed and wafted to the throne of God. Ascending smoke, descending flame, and the resultant sweep of revolutionary movement, indicate the *prevalence* of the prayers of all saints. Even change and upheaval, "voices, thunderings, lightnings, and an earthquake," are made to subserve the redeeming purposes of the Lord Jesus Christ. They are instrumental in the removal of obstacles. Forces of evil are by this means swept from the field, and a way prepared for the wider diffusion of the gospel. Through the costly Crimean war the gates of the Turkish empire were opened to Christianity. From the terrible Indian Mutiny dates a new era in the history of Eastern missionary enterprise. China was hermetically sealed, until the ironclads burst through the barriers of ages. Civil conflict led to the abolition of American slavery. Tel-el-Keber was the termination of the British campaign in Egypt, but only a starting-point for spiritual enterprise. Earthly movements sweep on to mediatorial consummation. The kingdoms of this world must become the kingdoms of our Lord, and of his Christ; and he shall reign for ever and ever. For this the Church pleads and waits: "Come forth out of thy royal chambers, O Prince of all the kings of the earth! Put on the robes of thy imperial Majesty; take up that unlimited sceptre which thy Almighty Father hath bequeathed thee; for now the voice of the bride calls thee, and all creatures sigh to be renewed."

Prayer on such a theme passes into praise. Three thousand years ago, unsurpassed missionary strains were chanted beneath the brightness of the Shekinah. The heart of the royal Psalmist was full of Christ, and longed its passion to declare: "He shall come down like rain upon the mown grass; as showers that water the earth. In his days shall the righteous flourish; and abundance of peace so long as the moon endureth. He shall have dominion also from sea to sea, and from the river to the ends of the earth."

The ground idea of this missionary hymn was doubtless suggested by the configuration or limits of Immanuel's land. But a resident of fair and favored Canada can scarcely help thinking of another special application. "From the river to the ends of the earth:" from the rolling floods of Niagara to the icy regions of the polar zone. "Dominion also!" Does not the name of this new northern nation seem to be prophetic of future and destined glory; a foremost place among the peoples that throng to the coronation of the heavenly King? "From sea to sea!" From coasts of Acadia, tidal deeps of the Bay of Fundy, and the majestic St. Lawrence, the jubilant strains shall rise; shall blend with the raptures of Ontario's lofty praise, break the silence of Lake Huron's shores, gather strength and volume from the peopled plains and prairies of Manitoba and the North-West, swell to the sources of the Saskatchewan and summits of the Rocky Mountains, gain tribute from the valleys and commercial gateways of British Columbia; and, as the voice of many waters, or the fulness of the deep, the gladness of salvation shall sound and spread "from sea to sea," from stormy Atlantic to bright and tranquil Pacific.

The missionary psalm was the latest as well as the loftiest ascription of the inspired bard. It was a magnificent

FINALE.

"The prayers of David the Son of Jesse are ended." No meaner subject could again rouse his spirit to sacred song. That harp of Judah has been long silent. But the sanctuary strain can never die. The rapture of praise to Christ shall fill the earth. "And he shall live, and to him shall be given of the gold of Sheba: prayer shall also be made for him continually; and daily shall he be praised."

> "People and realms of every tongue
> Dwell on his love with sweetest song."

"His name shall endure for ever: his name shall be continued as long as the sun: and men shall be blessed in him: all nations shall call him blessed. Blessed be the Lord God, the God of Israel, who only doeth wondrous things. And blessed be his glorious name for ever: and let the whole earth be filled with his glory. Amen and amen."

Passing years between, the eye rests upon "scenes of accomplished bliss." Promise and prophecy have been fulfilled. The world has been won for Christ.

> "One song employs all nations; and all cry,
> 'Worthy the Lamb, for he was slain for us!'
> The dwellers in the vales and on the rocks
> Shout to each other, and the mountain-tops
> From distant mountains catch the flying joy:
> Till, nation after nation taught the strain,
> Earth rolls the rapturous hosanna round."

Ascriptions of earth, born of missionary sympathy and prayer, are but the prelude of an eternal song. "After this I beheld, and lo a great multitude which no man could number, of all nations, and kindreds, and people, and tongues, stood before the throne, and before the Lamb, clothed with white robes, and palms in their hands; and cried with a loud voice, saying— SALVATION TO OUR GOD WHICH SITTETH UPON THE THRONE, AND UNTO THE LAMB."

APPENDIX.

Summaries and statistics are appended here for the sake of convenient reference.

1. AN ESTIMATE OF THE POPULATION OF THE WORLD, ACCORDING TO RELIGIONS,

given in the diagram at the front of this volume, was prepared for the Woman's Missionary Society of the Methodist Episcopal Church, and published by the Rev. Dr. Sutherland in *The Missionary Outlook.* The blocks are shaded to show the following religious divisions :—

Heathen	855	millions.
Mohammedans	170	"
Jews	8	"
Romanists	190	"
Greek Church	84	"
Protestants	116	"
Total	1,423	"

Another estimate, which in the main has been followed throughout the previous essay, was presented at the Cincinnati Convention. The aggregate, one thousand four hundred and thirty-three million, agrees with the round total of the eminent German statists for 1883:

Christians, including Protestants, Greek Church, and Roman Catholics, *plus*..	440 millions.
Jews	8 "
Moslems	175 "
Brahmans	160 "
Buddhists	400 "
Uncivilized Pagans	250 "
Total	1,433 "

Each square of the diagram, it will be seen, represents a million of population. As the result of faithful toil, an important space has brightened with the progress of the century. But a glance over the dark blocks shews the vast extent of heathendom, and the need of a greatly increased agency. To give one missionary to every 50,000 of the population, would require 20 for each square, or million of people. Brahmans, Buddhists, and heathens of yet uncivilized lands—without including Moslems—aggregate at least 810 squares, or millions; and to meet the demands of such an enterprise, up to the proportion specified, would require 16,200 missionaries—13,800 in addition to the 2,400 already in the field.

2. LATEST ESTIMATE OF THE WORLD'S POPULATION:—

Drs. Behm and Wagner have recently issued a new edition of their well-known collection of statistics—"Die Bevolkerung der Erde." They give the total as 1,433,887,500, which is about 22,000,000 less than their estimate of two years ago. They have concluded that China, including Corea, has 379,500,000, which is

55,000,000 less than they formerly supposed. There has thus been an actual increase of about 33,000,000 in the population of the globe—an increase, however, which must be spread over ten years, as many of the recent censuses are decennial. For Europe, the present population is rated at 327,743,400, showing an increase of about 12,000,000 over the previous figures by the operation of the censuses. In Asia, making allowance for the readjustment of the population of China, there has been an increase of 20,000,000, the present population being set down at 795,591,000. In Africa the population is 205,823,200. In America 100,415,400. In Australia and Polynesia, 4,232,000. In the Polar Regions, 82,500.—*Mis. Al., 1883, p. 15.*

3. Distribution of Foreign Missions.

We cull from Dr. Dorchester's tables the following statistics with reference to the distribution of Protestant Foreign Mission work in the different great divisions of the globe, in 1880, so far as reported:—

	Missions.	Principal Stations.	Sub-Stations.	Foreign and Native Ordained Ministers.	Lay Assistants.	Communicants.	Hearers or Adherents.
North America	83	951	1,214	1,602	3,328	211,833	332,054
South America	12	54	86	117	558	12,981	47,585
Europe	63	682	2,934	785	1,285	94,036	42,076
Africa	103	589	3,934	897	11,094	164,701	518,075
Asia	175	902	2,570	2,033	9,266	245,685	341,686
Oceanica	65	2,587	1,471	1,262	8,325	128,096	532,120
Total	504	5,765	12,209	6,696	33,856	857,332	1,813,596

Estimating for the Missions whose reports are not obtained in those items, Dr. Dorchester gave for the aggregate of "communicants" over 1,000,000, and of universal "adherents" from 3,000,000 to 3,500,000.—*The Gospel in all Lands, December, 1881.*

4. AMERICAN AND EUROPEAN SOCIETIES.

The Rev. Dr. Wilder, in the *Missionary Review* for Nov.-Dec., 1882, gives the following totals of 100 different Churches and Societies:—*American*—Home strength, 77,953 ministers and 10,165,976 communicants. Missionaries: ordained, 844; lay, 77; women, 978. Native workers: ordained, 839; others, 7,359. Native communicants, 197,102. *European*—Home strength, 39,746 ministers, 16,538,877 communicants. Missionaries: ordained, 1,756; lay, 548; women, 628. Native workers: ordained, 1,118; others, 14,730. Native communicants, 377,619. *Total*—Missionaries: ordained, 2,600; lay, 625; women, 1,606. Native workers: ordained, 1,957; others, 22,089. Native communicants, 574,721. Income, $8,447,991.—*Missionary Almanac, 1883, p. 15.*

BOOKS

PUBLISHED BY

WILLIAM BRIGGS,

78 & 80 KING STREET EAST,

TORONTO.

By the Rev. John Lathern.

The Macedonian Cry. A Voice from the Lands of Brahma and Buddha, Africa and Isles of the Sea, and A Plea for Missions. 12mo, cloth ....
The Hon. Judge Wilmot, late Lieut.-Governor of New Brunswick. A Biographical Sketch. Introduction by the Rev. D. D. Currie. With Artotype portrait. Cloth, 12mo... $0 75
Baptisma. Exegetical and Controversial. Cloth, 12mo 0 75

By the Rev. D. Rogers.

Shot and Shell for the Temperance Conflict. With an Introduction by the Rev. E. H. Dewart, D D. 12mo, 184 pp. With Illustrations. Bound in handsome style, in extra English cloth, with ink stamping and gold lettering 0 55

By the Rev. E. Barrass, M.A.

Smiles and Tears; or, Sketches from Real Life. With Introduction by the Rev. W. H. Withrow, D.D. Bound in cloth, gilt edges, extra gilt 0 50

By the Rev. J. Jackson Wray.

Matthew Mellowdew; A Story with More Heroes than One. Illustrated. Cloth, $1.00. Extra gilt 1 25

"In Matthew Mellowdew, the advantages and happiness of leading a Christian life are urged in an earnest and affecting style."—*Irish Times.*

Books Published by William Briggs,

Paul Meggit's Delusion. Illustrated. Cloth $1 00
> "A strong and heartily-written tale, conveying sound moral and religious lessons in an unobjectionable form."—*Graphic*.

Nestleton Magna; A Story of Yorkshire Methodism. Illustrated. Cloth 1 00
> "No one can read it without feeling better for its happy simple piety; full of vivacity, and racy of the genuine vernacular of the District."—*Watchman*.

By the Rev. W. H. Withrow, D.D.

Canadian in Europe. Being Sketches of Travel in France, Italy, Switzerland, Germany, Holland, Belgium, Great Britain, and Ireland. Illustrated. Cloth, 12mo 1 25

"Valeria," the Martyr of the Catacombs. A Tale of Early Christian Life in Rome. Illustrated. Cloth 0 75
> "The subject is skillfully handled, and the lesson it conveys is noble and encouraging."—*Daily Chronicle*.
> "A vivid and realistic picture of the times of the persecution of the Early Christians under Diocletian."—*Watchman*.
> "The Story is fascinatingly told, and conveys a vast amount of information."—*The Witness*.

Kings Messenger; or, Lawrence Temple's Probation 12mo, cloth 0 75
> "A capital story... We have seldom read a work of this kind with more interest, or one that we could recommend with greater confidence."—*Bible Christian Magazine*.

Neville Trueman, the Pioneer Preacher. A Tale of the War of 1812. 12mo, cloth. Illustrated 0 75
Methodist Worthies. Cloth, 12mo, 165 pp 0 60
Romance of Missions. Cloth, 12mo, 160 pp 0 60
Great Preachers. Ancient and Modern. Cloth, 12mo 0 60
Intemperance; Its Evils and their Remedies. Paper 0 15
Is Alcohol Food? Paper, 5c., per hundred 3 00
Prohibition the Duty of the Hour. Paper, 5c., per hundred. 3 00
The Bible and the Temperance Question. Paper 0 10
The Liquor Traffic. Paper 0 05
The Physiological Effects of Alcohol. Paper 0 10
Popular History of Canada. 600 pp., 8vo. Five Steel Engravings, and One Hundred Wood Cuts. Sold only by Subscription 3 00

By the Rev. J. S. Evans.

Christian Rewards; or, I. The Everlasting Rewards for Children Workers; II. The Antecedent Millennial Reward for Christian Martyrs. With notes:—1. True Christians may have Self-love but not Selfishness; 2. Evangelical Faith-works; 3. Justification by Faith does not include a Title to Everlasting Reward. 12mo, cloth 0 50

78 and 80 King St. East, Toronto.

In Press—The One Mediator. Selections and Thoughts on the Propitiatory Sacrifice and Intercessions of our Great High-Priest ....

By the Rev. Egerton Ryerson, D.D., LL.D.

Loyalists of America and Their Times. 2 Vols., large 8vo, with Portrait. Cloth, $5; half morocco $7 00
Canadian Methodism; Its Epochs and Characteristics. Handsomely bound in extra cloth, with Steel Portrait of the Author. 12mo, cloth, 440 pp 1 25
The Story of My Life. Edited by Rev. Dr. Nelles, Rev. Dr. Potts, and J. George Hodgins, Esq., LL.D. With Steel Portrait and Illustrations. (Sold only by Subscription.) Cloth, $3; sheep 4 00

By the Rev. J. Cynddylan Jones.

Studies in Matthew. 12mo, cloth. (Canadian Copyright Edition) 1 25
 "This is a remarkable volume of Sermons. The style, while severly logical, reminds us in its beauty and simplicity of Ruskin. These are models of what pulpit discourses ought to be."—*Methodist Recorder*.
Studies in Acts. 12mo, cloth 1 50
 "No exaggeration to say that Mr. Jones is fully equal to Robertson at his best, and not seldom superior to him."—*Methodist Recorder*.
In Preparation—Studies in Gospel of St. John.

By the Rev. Wm. Arthur, M.A.

Life of Gideon Ouseley, with Portrait. Cloth 1 00
All are Living. An attempt to Prove that the Soul while Separate from the Body is Consciously Alive. Each, 3c., per hundred 2 00
Did Christ Die for All? Each, 3c.; per hundred 2 00
Free, Full, and Present Salvation. Each, 3c.; per hundred.. 2 00
Heroes. A Lecture delivered before the Y.M.C.A. in Exeter Hall, London. Each, 5c.; per hundred 3 00
Is the Bible to Lie Under a Ban in India? A Question for Christian Electors. Each, 3c.; per hundred 2 00
May we Hope for a Great Revival. Each, 3c.; per hundred.. 2 00
Only Believe. Each, 3c.; per hundred 2 00
The Christian Raised to the Throne of Christ. Each, 3c.; per hundred 2 00
The Conversion of All England. Each, 3c.; per hundred.... 2 00
The Duty of Giving Away a Stated Portion of Your Income. each, 5c.; per hundred 3 00
The Friend whose Years do not Fail. Each, 3c.; per hundred 2 00

Books Published by William Briggs,

By the Rev. W. M. Punshon, D.D., LL.D.

Lectures and Sermons. Printed on thick superfine paper, 378 pp., with fine Steel Portrait, and strongly bound in extra fine cloth....	$1 00

This volume contains some of Dr. Punshon's grandest Lectures and Sermons, which have been listened to by tens of thousands who will remember them as brilliant productions from an acknowledged genius.

Canada and its Religious Prospects. Paper.	0 05
Memorial Sermons. Containing a Sermon, each, by Drs. Punshon, Gervase Smith, J. W. Lindsay, and A. P. Lowrey. Paper, 25c.; cloth	0 35
Tabor; or, The Class-meeting. A Plea and an Appeal. Paper, each 5c.; per dozen	0 30
The Prodigal Son, Four Discourses on. 87 pages. Paper, cover, 25c.; cloth	0 35
The Pulpit and the Pew: Their Duties to Each Other and to God. Two Addresses. Paper cover, 10c.; cloth	0 45

By the Rev. E. H. Dewart, D.D.

Broken Reeds; or, The Heresies of the Plymouth Brethern. New and enlarged edition	0 10
High Church Pretentions Disproved; or, Methodism and the Church of England	0 10
Living Epistles; or, Christ's Witnesses in the World. 12mo, cloth, 288 pp.	1 00

> Rev. Dr. A. C. George, in the New York *Christian Advocate*, says:—"These are, without exception, admirable essays, clear, earnest, logical, convincing, practical, and powerful. They are full of valuable suggestions for ministers, teachers, class-leaders, and all others who desire to present and enforce important biblical truths."

> The New York *Observer* says:—"The essays are practical, earnest, and warm, such as ought to do great good, and the one on Christianity and Scepticism is very timely and well put."

Misleading Lights. A Review of Current Antinomian Theories —The Atonement and Justification, 3c.; per dozen	0 30
Songs of Life. A Collection of Original Poems. Cloth	0 75
Spurious Catholicity. A Reply to the Rev. James Roy	0 10
The Development of Doctrine. Lecture delivered before the Theological Union, Victoria College	0 20
What is Arminianism? with a Brief Sketch of Arminius. By Rev. D. D. Whedon, D.D., LL.D., with Introduction by Dr. Dewart	0 10
Waymarks; or, Counsels and Encouragements to Penitent Seekers of Salvation, 5c.; per hundred	3 00

78 and 80 King St. East, Toronto.

By the Rev. J. C. Seymour.

The Temperance Battlefield and How to Gain the Day. Illustrated. 12mo, cloth $0 65
Voices from the Throne; or, God's Call to Faith and Obedience. Cloth 0 50

By the Rev. Alex. Sutherland, D.D.

A Summer in Prairie-Land. Notes of Tour through the North-West Territory. Paper, 40 cts.; cloth 0 70
Erring Through Wine....................................... 0 05

By the Rev. George H. Cornish.

Cyclopædia of Methodism in Canada. Containing Historical, Educational, and Statistical Information, dating from the beginning of the work in the several Provinces in the Dominion of Canada, with Portrait and Illustrations. Cloth, $4.50; sheep.................................... 5 00
Pastor's Record and Pocket Ritual. Russia limp, 75 cents. Roan, with flap and pocket 0 90

By the Rev. W. J. Hunter, D.D.

The Pleasure Dance and its Relation to Religion and Morality. 0 10
Popular Amusements 0 10

By John Ashworth.

Strange Tales from Humble Life. First series. 12mo, 470 pp., cloth 1 00
Strange Tales from Humble Life. Second series, cloth 0 45

By the Rev. H. F. Bland.

Soul-Winning. A Course of Four Lectures delivered at Victoria University 0 30
Universal Childhood Drawn to Christ. With an Appendix containing remarks on the Rev. Dr. Burwash's "Moral Condition of Childhood." Paper..... .... 0 10

5

Books Published by William Briggs,

By the Rev. John Carroll, D.D.

Case and His Contemporaries. A Biographical History of Methodism in Canada. 5 vols., cloth..................	$4 90
Father Corson; being the Life of the late Rev. Robert Corson. 12mo, cloth..	0 90
"My Boy Life." Presented in a Succession of True Stories. 12mo, cloth, 300 pp.................................	1 00
Methodist Baptism. Paper	0 10
Exposition Expounded, Defended and Supplemented. Limp cloth	0 40
School of the Prophets, Father McRorey's Class, and Squire Firstman's Kitchen Fire...........................	0 75

By the Rev. S. G. Phillips, M.A.

The Evangelical Denominations of the Age	0 15
The Need of the World. With Introduction by the Rev. S. S. Nelles, D.D., LL.D. Cloth......................	1 00
In Press—The Methodist Pulpit. A Collection of Original Sermons from Living Ministers of the United Methodist Church in Canada. Edited by the Rev. S. G. Phillips ..	

By the Rev. Hugh Johnston, M.A., B.D.

Toward the Sunrise. Being Sketches of Travel in the East. Illustrated. To which is added a Memorial Sketch of Rev. W. M. Punshon, LL.D., with Portrait. 460 pp., 12mo, cloth	1 25
The Practical Test of Christianity. A Sermon delivered before the Theological Union, Victoria College, 1883	0 20

Applied Logic. By the Rev. S. S. Nelles, LL.D. Cloth....	$0 75
Arrows in the Heart of the King's Enemies; or, Atheistic Errors of the Day Refuted, and the Doctrine of a Personal God Vindicated. By the Rev. Alexander W. McLeod, D.D. formerly editor of the *Wesleyan*, Halifax, N.S., 12mo, cloth	0 45

78 and 80 King St. East, Toronto.

Burial in Baptism. A Colloquy, in which the Claims of Ritual Baptism in Romans vi. 3, 4, Colossians ii. 12 are examined and Shown to be Visionary. By the Rev. T. L. Wilkinson. Paper, 5c.; per hundred................. $3 00
Catechism of Baptism. By the Rev. D. D. Currie. Cloth... 0 50
Certainties of Religion. By the Rev. J. A. Williams, D.D., F.T.L., and The Soul's Anchor. By the Rev. George McRitchie.. 0 20
Christian Perfection. By the Rev. J. Wesley. Paper, 10c.; cloth 0 20
Church Membership; or, The Conditions of New Testament and Methodist Church Membership Examined and Compared. By the Rev. S. Bond, Methodist Minister of the Montreal Conference. 18mo, cloth, 72 pp. 0 35
Circuit Register 1 50
Class-Leader, The; His Work and How to Do it. By J. Atkinson, M.A. Cloth, 12mo, cheap edition 0 60

> "It is practical, sprightly, devout, and full of profit. We would urge every class-leader to possess himself of a copy."—*Christian Guardian.*

Class-Meeting, The. Its Spiritual Authority and Practical Value. By the Rev. J. A. Chapman, M.A 0 10
Conversations on Baptism. By the Rev. Alexander Langford, Cloth 0 30
Companion to the Revised New Testament. By Alexander Roberts, D.D., and an American Reviser. Paper, 30c.; cloth 0 65
The Life of Alexander Duff, D.D., LL.D. By George Smith, C.J.E., LL.D., Author of "The Life of John Wilson, D.D., F.R.S.," Fellow of the Royal Geographical and Statistical Society, &c., with an Introduction by Wm. M. Taylor, D.D. Two large octavo volumes, bound in cloth, with Portraits by Jeens 3 00
Journal of the General Conference, for the years 1874, 1878, and 1882. Paper, 60c.; cloth 0 75
Journal of First United General Conference, 1883. Paper, 70c.; cloth 1 00
Lectures and Sermons. Delivered before the "Theological Union" of the University of Victoria College. 1879 to 1882 inclusive, in one volume, cloth................... 0 75
The above may be had separately, in paper covers, each.. 0 20
Librarian's Account Book 0 50
Life and Times of Anson Green, D.D. Written by himself. 12mo, cloth, with Portrait............................ 1 00
Lone Land Lights. By the Rev. J. McLean. Cloth........ 0 35
Memories of James B. Morrow. By the Rev. A. W. Nicholson. Cloth 0 75

Books Published by William Briggs.

Memorials of Mr. and Mrs. Jackson. With Steel Portrait. Cloth	$0 35
Methodist Catechisms. No. 1., per dozen, 25c.; No. II., per dozen, 60c.; No III., per dozen, 75c. Three in one. Cloth. Each	0 25
Methodist Hymn-Books. In various sizes and styles of binding. Prices from 30 cents upwards.	
Old Christianity against Papal Novelties. By Gideon Ouseley, Illustrated. Cloth	1 00
Prayer and its Remarkable Answers. By W. W. Patton, D.D. Cloth	1 00
Recreations. A Book of Poems. By the Rev. E. A. Stafford, M.A., President of the Montreal Conference. It is beautifully printed on English paper, and bound in extra English cloth, bevelled edges, and lettered in gold	0 35
Religion of Life; or, Christ and Nicodemus. By John G. Manly. Cloth	0 50

"Of the orthodox evangelical type, vigorous and earnest. Most great theological questions come up for more or less of notice, and Mr. Manly's remarks are always thoughtful and penetrating."—*The British Quarterly Review.*

Roll Book. Designed for the Use of Infant Classes. One-quire Book containing lines for 178 Scholars, and lasting for 13 years, $1.00; and a Two-quire Book similar to above	1 50
Secretary's Minute Book. New design. By Thomas Wallis. Boards	0 60
Secretary's Minute Book	0 50
Sermons on Christian Life. By the Rev. C. W. Hawkins. Cloth	1 00
Spiritual Struggles of a Roman Catholic. An Autobiographical Sketch. By the Rev. Louis N. Beaudry. Steel Portrait. Cloth	1 00

"We do not remember having seen a volume better fitted than this for universal circulation among Protestants and Romanists."—*Talmage's Christian at Work.*

Sunday-School Class Book. Cloth, per dozen	0 75
Sunday-School Class Book. New design. Cloth, per doz	1 50
Sunday-School Register	0 50
Sunday-School Record (new) for Secretaries	1 25
Theological Compend. By the Rev. Amos Binney. 32mo, cloth	0 30
The Guiding Angel. By Kate Murray. 18mo, cloth	0 30
Weekly Offering Book	1 50
Within the Veil; or, Entire Sanctification. By the Rev. Jas. Caswell	0 10

☞ *Any Book mailed post-free on receipt of price.*

www.ingramcontent.com/pod-product-compliance
Lightning Source LLC
Chambersburg PA
CBHW032107230426
43672CB00009B/1659